The Rise and Fall of the 5 Empires in the Bible

The Rise and Fall of the 5 Empires in the Bible

278-3, Nonhyeon-dong,
Gangnam-gu, Seoul, Korea (06103)
http://www.tongbooks.com

Printed in South Korea

ISBN 978-89-85738-84-2 03230

The Rise and Fall of the 5 Empires in the Bible

Byoungho Zoh

Tongdokwon

Contents

Introduction **BIBLE with EGYPT**

Chapter 1 BIBLE with ASSYRIAN EMPIRE

Chapter 2 BIBLE with BABYLONIAN EMPIRE

Chapter 3 BIBLE with PERSIAN EMPIRE

Chapter 4 BIBLE with HELLENISTIC EMPIRE

Chapter 5 BIBLE with ROMAN EMPIRE

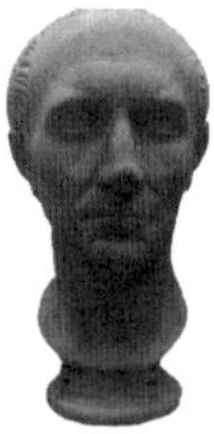

Introduction

For over thirty years, I have been studying and teaching the Bible. One of the reasons I am passionate in learning and sharing God's Word is because it shows me a God who loves, forgives, delivers, redeems, cares for, takes care of, and listens to His people. The Bible is not just a collection of stories, prose, or rules. It's the beautiful and universal language of God given to us to guide our lives in His ways. The Bible is timeless and is relevant to us not only in our individual lives, but also for our family, our nation, and every nation. When we commit ourselves to studying the Scriptures and applying it to our daily lives, we increase our faith, gain wisdom, and discover how and why we must follow God, not the world.

I am particularly fascinated with how world history is interwoven in the Bible through the ancient empires. When I hear people comment that they believe the Bible is a myth or a fairytale storybook, I find the evidence of the empires as written in God's Word one way to prove its authenticity. Though references outside of the Bible are necessary to study world history, I believe the Bible is the number one source to learn about the world's past as well as her present and future.

It is my heart's desire to show others how they can learn about history through a spiritual lens. This motivation is what led me to write *The Rise and Fall of the Five Empires in the Bible*. In this book, I explore one 'almost' and five full-scale empires and what I believe are the keywords that describe their way of governing, or their empire in general - Egypt (Mother Nature), Assyria (boundary), Babylon (education), Persia (numbers), Hellenistic (amalgamate), and Rome (tolerance). I also explore the genesis and the division of ancient Israel and her relationship with each of these empires in history.

Through reading about the rise and fall of these powerful empires, you'll see how most of the leaders of these nations were led by greed and selfish desires - not by God - to conquer more land by force or bloodshed. The nation of Israel, however, was held to a higher standard, a standard that required them to follow God. Throughout this book, you'll see how the Israelites vacillated between honoring God and following the world. Their biggest mistake - as can be ours today - was putting their trust in mighty powers instead of trusting solely in God.

When we study these ancient powers, we see the vast difference between empires established through human endeavors and those established by God. While empires vanish into the shadow of history, the kingdom of God is eternal. This message was an important lesson not only for the people of ancient Israel, but it's just as important to us today.

It is my hope that as you read this book, you will learn not only about the role of these ancient empires in world history, but gain an understanding into how we must live our lives as an individual and as leaders and followers of Christ. May this book teach you that there is nothing greater than the love, power, might, and grace of God. May this book show you that God cares about and only wants the best for His children. May this book remind you that though kingdoms rise and fall, it is the Lord, and only Him, who will last forever.

*All Scripture quotations listed are from the Holy Bible, New International Version (NIV)

The Rise and Fall of the 5 Empires in the Bible

PRESTUDY
BIBLE with EGYPT

The books of the Bible related to Egypt

Genesis, Exodus, Leviticus,
Numbers, Deuteronomy, Joshua etc.

Egypt Yesterday and Egypt Today

On January 25, 2011, the world watched with baited breath as the people of Egypt launched a massive uprising and revolution. Global media outlets reported the news live every hour every day for eighteen days. Journalists were injured in the mayhem that erupted in the streets while millions of protestors demanded that Egyptian President Hosni Mubarak step down from office. Until that time, Mubarak had not garnered much attention as the leader of the African country. In fact, it wasn't well known that during his thirty - year rule, the Egyptians were marked by poverty, destruction, and despair. After two and a half weeks of protests, the president resigned.

The victory of this democratic revolution was far-reaching and ignited sparks that spread throughout Africa and the Arab world. I think this was perhaps the first time that Egypt had drawn the attention of the world since the Exodus thirty-four hundred years ago.

With over twelve million visitors in 2008, Egypt is a popular tourist destination today. People all over the world travel there to see the remains of the famous ancient structures and monuments of the ancient civilization like the Great Sphinx at Giza, the Abu Simbel temples, and the Valley of the Kings near Luxor. Egypt has made numerous contributions to the art world, too. Many international countries, especially in Europe, display Egyptian artifacts in their museums, including the renowned British Museum.

Egypt is and has always been an extraordinary country. As early as twentieth century BC, it was a leader in agriculture, a cutting-edge industry at the time. Egyptians were credited with building the first chariot and for constructing incredible architectural edifices like the awe-inspiring pyramids.

The economy of ancient Egypt flourished with the introduction of a million plus Hebrew slaves as labor power. You could say that Egypt's financial success was attributed to the Hebrew population because they worked to the bone for the country for no wage. Their contribution must not be forgotten.

The fifth century BC Greek historian Herodotus said, "Egypt is a gift of the Nile." This statement was true at that time and still is today. Like ancient China and India, countries who built their civilizations around big rivers, Egypt did the same around the Nile River. This fertile valley offered the country additional sources of economic prosperity. The Nile also played an important role in the ancient Near East and also Mesopotamia. As you continue to read this book, you'll see how abundant Egypt was and why the five Biblical empires fought to occupy her.

Fast forward to 2011. The picture of Egypt shown on media everywhere depicted a country nowhere near as prosperous as it was centuries ago. In the twenty-first century, it became a pitiful country suffering from a serious economic crisis. Thirty percent of the Egyptian population was unemployed; young people made up eighty percent of that number.[1)]

When I was writing the outline for this book, I thought about adding

Egypt as an empire. I came to the conclusion, however, that there are some limitations that prevent me from being able to describe her as a full-scale empire. First, she did not have the lasting military manpower as the other five empires. When Moses led the Hebrew slaves out of Egypt during the Exodus, the impressive military army of Egypt could not withstand the destructive power of the Red Sea. Everyone, from a foot soldier to a general, drowned in the miraculous event, and the imposing arsenal of Egypt's weapons were consequently destroyed. Second, Egypt was eventually occupied by Babylon, and subsequently the Persian, Greek, and Roman empires. Nevertheless, before we study the five empires, it's important and worthwhile to look at Egypt because of her rich and socially complex early civilization.

The historical account written in the book of Genesis takes place in Egypt. God had a specific role and purpose for that country in the lives of the Hebrew people. He ordered Jacob and his family to go down to Egypt and promised that He would make them a great nation and that they would one day return to Canaan, the Promised Land(see Genesis 46:3-4).

Pharaoh the King
The British Museum

Sure enough, as time passed, the Hebrew people journeyed to Egypt to settled their families and multiplied in number. "But the Israelites were fruitful and multiplied greatly and became exceedingly numerous, so that the land was filled with them"(Exodus 1:7). Their numbers became so great that the Egyptian nation felt threatened. Pharaoh said to his people, "The Israelites have become far too numerous for us"(Exodus 1:9). Although the country was teeming with economic abundance, the Hebrews became an obstacle to Egypt's dream of expanding into an empire.

Pharaoh wanted to do something about this thorn in his side so he formulated a plan. He initially forced the Hebrew people to become slaves to Egypt and, in a later desperate measure, issued an order to have all baby boys killed at birth. "When you help the Hebrew women in childbirth and observe them on the delivery stool, if it is a boy, kill him; but if it is a girl, let her live"(Exodus 1:16). Pharaoh did not want an eventual uprising of young men to form a coup with surrounding nations while the Egyptian military was away at battle and, therefore, unable to defend the country.

When Moses showed up to represent the Hebrew people and lead them into freedom, he ultimately thwarted Pharaoh's cruel and unjust attempts to expand his kingdom. At first, Moses didn't pose much of a threat to Pharaoh. The king didn't even blink when Moses came on the scene. But after some time, it was clear the conflict between the Hebrews and Egyptians was not to be taken lightly. The battle was akin to the one between David and Goliath, with the Hebrews playing the role of underdog David.

When God, through Moses, finally brought His people out of Egypt in the historic Exodus, the vivid display of God's authority, power, and glory became international news and moved people all over the world to recognize God's supremacy both in heaven and on earth. The news even reached the ears of the prostitute Rahab years later.

In the story of the two spies written in the book of Joshua, Rahab told the Israelite men, "I know that the Lord has given this land to you and that a great fear of you has fallen on us, so that all who live in this country are melting in fear because of you. We have heard how the Lord dried up the water of the Red Sea for you when you came out of Egypt, and what you did to Sihon and Og, the two kings of the Amorites east of the Jordan, whom you completely destroyed. When we heard of it, our hearts melted and everyone's courage failed because of you, for the Lord your God is God in heaven above and on the earth below. Now then, please swear to me by the Lord that you will show kindness to my family, because I have shown kindness to you. Give me a sure sign"(Joshua 2:9-12).

I believe the Exodus, the dissolution of the Egyptian army, and the country's subsequent fall would have made headline news today in the same manner as the 2011 revolution did.

Nationalism and Imperialism

The Bible speaks of the word "nation" right in its opening book, Genesis. God told Abraham he would form a "nation" out of him and that He would bless all nations through that one nation(see Genesis 12:2). Note God didn't say He would create a family, which is what you might normally think of being created out of one person. The God who created the universe was clear. He would establish a nation through one man, Abraham. This was a miraculous promise because at the time, the Hebrews weren't many in number.

Generally, a nation refers to a group of people who are connected to each other culturally and regionally. According to [dictionary.com] it means "a large body of people, associated with a particular territory, that is sufficiently conscious of its unity to seek or to possess a government peculiarly its own." In the Bible, the word "nation" is mentioned many times before its actual existence. Even when Rebekah, the wife of Isaac, the son of Abraham, conceived twin boys, God told her, "Two nations are in your womb, and two peoples from within you will be separated"(Genesis 25:23). True to His Word, one twin, Jacob, came to form the nation of Israel and the other twin, Esau, formed the nation of Edom. God's mention of "nation" is evidence to His ownership of all countries, nations, and land, which He asserted from the beginning of time. "...The whole earth is mine"(Exodus 19:5).

All this about nations tells us that God is concerned with not only the individual person but with families, nations, and the whole world. There are many references to this fact in the Scriptures. It is even the core message in the New Testament. When Jesus left earth to return to heaven, He said, "Therefore, go and make disciples of all nations..."(Matthew 28:19).

Let's talk about nationalism, an ideology or a movement that promotes the unity, independence, and prosperity of a nation.[2] In a broad sense, the current struggles for democracy in Egypt and across the Arab world are a form of nationalism. Attaching "ism" to an ideology, whatever it may be - individualism, materialism, nationalism - signifies that the ideology has become an important part of the nation's belief system and that it can have a profound effect on existing cultural mores and behaviors.

Nationalism isn't a bad thing in and of itself. It can, however, become injurious when it starts to negatively affect other people and countries. Loyalty and patriotism, which form the basis for nationalism, can lead to feelings of superiority, which can lead to political and economic bullying.

The book of Genesis gives an example of how nationalism can cause offense. There is a scene in Genesis 43 where Joseph, appointed the vizier of Egypt by Pharaoh, sees his family for the first time since they had sold him into slavery years earlier. There was a severe famine in Egypt, Canaan, and all over the world. Joseph was selling grain, and people from different nations were coming to him to buy some. Before Joseph's brothers knew who he was, they appeared before him begging for food. Through a series of interesting events, they find themselves eating in Joseph's house.

When the elaborate meal is laid out, Joseph and the other Egyptian men with him are served separately, apart from his brothers(see Genesis 43:32). Joseph wasn't being purposely rude or making a show of his pride. In that culture, it was offensive for Egyptians to eat with Hebrews.

Being proud of your country is important, and a good thing, but when it goes too far other nations and races can suffer and become fearful. Patriotic and superior feelings can take a negative turn and transform nationalism into imperialism. Empires formed through imperialism pose a threat to other nations. These empires disregard the sovereignty of other nations, refuse to recognize land boundaries, and rule their people and others through domination.

In the days of the Roman Republic, those who held the highest military and judicial authority over a territory were granted *imperium*, or absolute power. It's where we get the term emperor. It is also the basis for the concept of building empires to attain power. When a country desires to expand into an empire through imperialism, the surrounding countries are faced with an immediate threat to their security. In the past, empires were known for invading and occupying other countries with advanced military force; today they are known for expansion through economic power.

Statue of King David
by Nicolas Cordier in the Borghese Chapel of the Basilica di Santa Maria Maggiore

There are many reasons David in the Bible was known as a great king. One reason is that he did not seek to enlarge the territory of Israel and make it an empire. During his rule, the nation had 1.3 million men who were able to fight in its army, and so it easily could have become a military powerhouse. "Joab reported the number of the fighting men to the king; In Israel there were eight hundred thousand able-bodied men who could handle a sword, and in Judah five hundred thousand"(2 Samuel 24:9). With such a large army, David had the potential and manpower to dominate other nations and become an empire as powerful as Assyria. God, however, was specific in the territory Israel could occupy as given through Moses. David respected those boundaries, and God respected him for it.

The boundary of Canaan God initially gave to the nation of Israel stretched from Lebo Hamath to the Wadi of Egypt(see 1 Kings 8:65) or from "Dan to Beersheba." The latter term was a common phrase used to describe the whole land of Israel inhabited during Biblical times. Dan was in the north, and Beersheba was in the south.

Imperialism and the Kingdom of Priests

Many times in the Bible, God refers to King David as "my servant David." This sign of affection and God's love for him had to do with the fact that David tried to carry out the task of the kingdom of priests.[3] What do empires and the kingdom of priests have to do with one another? "Kingdom of priests" is an important concept that God spoke about since the beginning of time.

The specific laws that describe, guide, and manage a kingdom of priests are found in the book of Leviticus. You must read it in order to fully understand this concept. You also will understand how the empires discussed in this book did not abide by the laws of God and, therefore, were not known as kingdoms of priests.

Long ago, God told Abraham that he would form a nation out of him that would become a channel of blessing for all nations. "I will make you into a great nation and I will bless you: I will make your name great, and you will be a blessing. I will bless those who bless you, and whoever curses you I will curse: and all peoples on earth will be blessed through

Moses is holding the Ten Commandments _by Rembrandt

you"(Genesis 12:2-3).

Five hundred years later, God said through Moses, "Now if you obey me fully and keep my covenant, then out of all nations you will be my treasured possession. Although the whole earth is mine, you will be for me a kingdom of priests and a holy nation. These are the words you are to speak to the Israelites"(Exodus 19:5-6). In this passage of Scripture, God specifically mentions the phrase "kingdom of priests."

The terms "empire" and "kingdom of priests" both revolve around nations. A kingdom of priests, however, is led by the laws of God and is obedient to His ways, not the ways of the world or a powerful authority not of God. While the underlying characteristics of an empire usually surround greed and an insatiable hunger for power, the intentions of a kingdom of priests are to serve and follow God.

Leviticus tells us, "If you follow my decrees and are careful to obey my commands...five of you will chase a hundred and a hundred of you will chase ten thousand, and your enemies will fall by the sword before you... You will still be eating last year's harvest when you will have to move it out to make room for the new"(Leviticus 26:3,8,10). God was saying that if His people managed the country according to His laws, namely according to the method of the kingdom of priests, God would be their defense and take care of them financially. This established covenant is important to us today. God will always take care of those who love and obey Him.

Empires, on the other hand, create turmoil and conflict in and out of their land. They usually invade other countries with the purpose of domination. They steal from others simply to become bigger, stronger, and richer. This is not God's way of doing things. The prophets in the Old Testament regularly mention that living according to the kingdom of priests is what pleases God and is how a nation should run. This is also key to fending off threatening empires.

More on Joseph

Joseph played a significant role in the prosperity of ancient Egypt. His life and his contribution to the country's well-being received the full attention of Biblical writers. Joseph was the eleventh son of his father Jacob, and was the favorite. Joseph's brothers were very jealous and one day devised a plan to kidnap and sell him into slavery. Joseph spent most of his adult life as an Egyptian slave. He had a series of ups and downs, including being falsely accused of rape and consequently being thrown into prison. In an unusual twist of events, many years after his brothers sold him, Joseph was appointed the vizier, or prime minister, of Egypt.

In his book, *A History of the Jews*, Paul Johnson described Joseph with much praise.

> "Joseph was the great minister-statesman of an alien ruler, the pattern of many Jews over the next 3,000 years. He was clever, quick, perceptive, imaginative; a dreamer, but more than a dreamer, a man with the creative ability to interpret complex phenomena, to forecast and foresee, to plan and administer. Quiet, industrious, able in all economic and financial affairs, the master also of many forms of arcane knowledge, he knew well how to serve power and exploit it on behalf of his people."[4]

Joseph Interprets Pharaoh's Dream
by Jean Adrien Guignet

Joseph's ride to power began with him interpreting a particularly disturbing dream for the king of Egypt(see Genesis 41). "When two full years had passed, Pharaoh had a dream: He was standing by the Nile, when out of the river there came up seven cows, sleek and fat, and they grazed among the reeds. After them, seven other cows, ugly and gaunt, came up out of the Nile and stood beside those on the riverbank. And the cows that were ugly and gaunt ate up the seven sleek, fat cows. Then Pharaoh woke up. He fell asleep again and had a second dream: Seven heads of grain, healthy and good, were growing on a single stalk. After them, seven other heads of grain sprouted - thin and scorched by the east wind. The thin heads of grain swallowed up the seven healthy, full heads. Then Pharaoh woke up; it had been a dream. In the morning his mind was troubled, so he sent for all the magicians and wise men of Egypt. Pharaoh told them his dreams, but no one could interpret them for him"(Genesis 4:1-8).

Desperate, Pharaoh approached Joseph, who was unjustly imprisoned in the palace at the time. The Hebrew prisoner explained the dream, saying Egypt would enjoy seven years of abundance and then suffer from a severe seven-year famine. Joseph then offered the king some advice:

> "And now let Pharaoh look for a discerning and wise man and put him in charge of the land of Egypt. Let Pharaoh appoint commissioners over the land to take a fifth of the harvest of Egypt during the seven years of abundance. They should collect all the food of these good years that are coming and store up the grain under the authority of Pharaoh, to be kept in the cities for food. This food should be held in reserve for the country, to be used during the seven years of famine that will come upon Egypt, so that the country may not be ruined by the famine"(Genesis 41:33-36).

Joseph's strategy worked. Saving one-fifth of harvest was the perfect amount. Two-fifths would have been too much, one-tenth too little.

I imagine the conversation must have been a little awkward. Just imagine the number one leader of Egypt approaching a prisoner for help; Pharaoh must have been very desperate. The fact that the king accepted Joseph's solution was a miracle in itself. He could have taken great offense with Joseph's prediction of hard times and punished him. That Joseph was trusted and appointed on the spot to a position of great power speaks volumes about how God can work wonders in unlikely situations. "Then Pharaoh said to Joseph, "Since God has made all this known to you, there is no one so discerning and wise as you. You shall be in charge of my palace, and all my people are to submit to your orders. Only with respect to the throne will I be greater than you"(Genesis 41:39-40).

Though Joseph didn't have an easy life, God obviously had a plan that allowed Joseph to benefit from everything he had learned during his life. For instance, Joseph became knowledgeable about stock farming as a young boy; he learned about agriculture when he worked at Potiphar's house before his imprisonment; and he came to understand prison administration when he was behind bars. Without these experiences and knowledge, Joseph could have never given Pharaoh such a smart answer.

Nor could he have reigned as Pharaoh's right-hand man with as much success, prestige, and wisdom as he did.

I think it's interesting to know how Joseph got his stock farming brains. In Genesis, we find that his father Jacob was owed some money from his uncle Laban and asked to be paid in sheep. "Let me go through all your flocks today and remove from them every speckled or spotted sheep, every dark-colored lamb and every spotted or speckled goat. They will be my wages"(Genesis 30:32). Then Jacob did something strange, yet very effective.

> He "took fresh-cut branches from poplar, almond and plane trees and made white stripes on them by peeling the bark and exposing the white inner wood of the branches. Then he placed the peeled branches in all the watering troughs, so that they would be directly in front of the flocks when they came to drink. When the flocks were in heat and came to drink, they mated in front of the branches. And they bore young that were streaked or speckled or spotted. Jacob set apart the young of the flock by themselves, but made the rest face the streaked and dark-colored animals that belonged to Laban. Thus he made separate flocks for himself and did not put them with Laban's animals. Whenever the stronger females were in heat, Jacob would place the branches in the troughs in front of the animals so they would mate near the branches, but if the animals were weak, he would not place them there. So the weak animals went to Laban and the strong ones to Jacob. In this way the man grew exceedingly prosperous and came to own large flocks, and female and male servants, and camels and donkeys"(Genesis 30:37-43).

What a genius!

It's easy to see why Joseph was so successful in the role of vizier. He contributed greatly to the prosperous state of Egypt's economy and to the riches Pharaoh accumulated. Here's one example. At Joseph's recommendation, the palace had spent much of the treasury buying the people's agricultural harvests, but when famine came Joseph was able to sell the stored grain at a high price, adding more money to the treasury and making Pharaoh even wealthier.

> "There was no food, however, in the whole region because the famine was severe; both Egypt and Canaan wasted away because of the famine. Joseph collected all the money that was to be found in Egypt and Canaan in payment for the grain they were buying, and he brought it to Pharaoh's palace"(Genesis 47:13-14).

When the people ran out of money, they started selling their land to Joseph in exchange for food. "So Joseph bought all of the land in Egypt for Pharaoh. All of the people of Egypt sold their fields. They did that because there wasn't enough food anywhere. In that way, the land became Pharaoh's"(Genesis 47:20). The Egyptian government could have easily been on its way to becoming an empire with its increasing wealth.

Joseph established a law that remained in effect for fifteen hundred years, until the rule of Roman Emperor Octavius. "Joseph said to the people, 'Now that I have bought you and your land today for Pharaoh, here is seed for you so you can plant the ground. But when the crop comes in, give a fifth of it to Pharaoh. The other four-fifths you may keep as seed for the fields and as food for yourselves and your households and your children'" (Genesis 47:23-24).

The Egyptians gratefully complied with Joseph's law. "You have saved our lives," they said. "May we find favor in the eyes of our lord; we will be in bondage to Pharaoh"(Genesis 47:25). Through the enacting of this law, Pharaoh accumulated even more wealth and land. The only land that did

Jacob's Body is taken to Canaan
by James Tissot

not become his possession was the land of the priests(see Genesis 47:26).

The country was in the second year of famine when Joseph's estranged family came to Egypt. It was also his ninth year as prime minister. God's plan was unfolding, as He had revealed to Jacob(see Genesis 46:3-4).

After Joseph made himself known to his family, he requested that his family move to Egypt. Wanting his family to maintain a separate identity from the Egyptians, Joseph coached them on how to respond to any questions. When asked by Pharaoh what they did for work, the brothers were told to say they tended livestock, just like their ancestors(see Genesis 46:34). This was important because the Egyptians looked down on shepherds, thus ensuring that Joseph's family would get to settle apart from the Egyptians in the region of Goshen and be prosperous within their own family, as God had promised. I like to think that Joseph's decision to have his family confess their livelihood as shepherds was intentional, so he could be responsible for and look after his family until their great nation was established.

Because of his wisdom and excellent leadership, clearly evidenced by delivering the Egyptians out of famine, Joseph was greatly respected by Pharaoh and the people. When Joseph's father died, it was considered a

Machpelah Cave Church in Hebron

national affair because the people thought of Joseph as a national hero. People mourned for Jacob for days(see Genesis 50:3). The funeral was an epic event, as a large party of family members and Egyptians officials traveled with Joseph to bury Jacob in Canaan. It was a foreshadowing of what would happen during the Exodus.[5]

> "So Joseph went up to bury his father. All Pharaoh's officials accompanied him - the dignitaries of his court and all the dignitaries of Egypt - besides all the members of Joseph's household and his brothers and those belonging to his father's household. Only their children and their flocks and herds were left in Goshen. Chariots and horsemen also went up with him. It was a very large company. When they reached the threshing floor of Atad, near the Jordan, they lamented loudly and bitterly; and there Joseph observed a seven-day period of mourning for his father. When the Canaanites who lived there saw the mourning at the threshing floor of Atad, they said, "The Egyptians are holding a solemn ceremony of mourning." That is why that place near the Jordan is called Abel Mizraim. So Jacob's sons did as he had commanded them: They carried him to the land of Canaan and buried him in the cave in the field of Machpelah, near Mamre, which Abraham had bought along with the field as a burial place from Ephron the Hittite. After burying his father, Joseph returned to Egypt, together with his brothers and all the others who had gone with him to bury his father"(Genesis 50:7-14).

Time passed and Joseph also died. He lived a meaningful life for both his family and the nation of Egypt. Even his bones had significance. Four hundred years later, his bones were excavated, carried during the Exodus, and buried in the land of Shechem, as Joseph had requested to the Israelites before he died. "...God will surely come to your aid, and then you must carry my bones up from this place"(Genesis 50:25). Joseph did not want his bones to rest in a grave until the nation of Israel had conquered Canaan and fulfilled God's promise.

When the Israelites reached the Promised Land, they remembered the words of Joseph. "And Joseph's bones, which the Israelites had brought up from Egypt, were buried at Shechem in the tract of land that Jacob bought for a hundred pieces of silver from the sons of Hamor, the father of Shechem. This became the inheritance of Joseph's descendants"(Joshua 24:32).

Enter Moses, the Prince of Egypt

The book of Exodus opens with a new king of Egypt. He didn't know Joseph nor did he look upon the Hebrew people with favor as Pharaoh had. His disdain for God's people is what led to the forced enslavement and eventual liberation of the Hebrew people. The mood at the end of the book of Genesis and the beginning of the book of Exodus is quite different. The tension is immediately obvious in the first chapter of Exodus.

The growing population of the Hebrews was a source of contention for the new king, Thutmose I, also referred to as Pharaoh. He was starting to feel nervous and even threatened by them. The first signs of Egypt's ambition to become an empire was seen when the king took drastic measures to reduce the number of Hebrew people.

The king told his people, "Come, we must deal shrewdly with them

or they will become even more numerous and, if war breaks out, will join our enemies, fight against us and leave the country"(Exodus 1:10). His first step was to force the Hebrews into manual labor. He ordered them to build supply cities, Pithom and Rameses, and gave them backbreaking tasks that would oppress them physically and spiritually. The king's plan didn't work. The Hebrew population still grew.

Pharaoh then enforced a drastic measure that he commanded the Hebrew midwives to carry out. "When you are helping the Hebrew women during childbirth on the delivery stool, if you see that the baby is a boy, kill him; but if it is a girl, let her live"(Exodus 1:16). The midwives, however, feared God more than the king and let the baby boys live(see verse 17).

The king did not give up. The government took matters into its own hands and ordered that all male babies be thrown into the Nile River. While these atrocities were going on, Moses was born. Most of us are familiar with his story - from his mother who couldn't bear to watch her son be killed so she hid him in a basket and placed him in the river; to Pharaoh's daughter finding the basket and showing compassion to the beautiful baby; to Moses becoming a prince in the king's palace; to Moses on the run after murdering an Egyptian who was abusing a Hebrew slave; to God calling Moses to lead His people out of bondage and into the Promised Land, the land of Canaan. (You can read all the details about his up-

Statue of Ramses II
The British Museum

bringing and background in the first chapters of Exodus.)

A lot of drama, to say the least, occurred between Moses and Pharaoh. I like to wonder what the initial conversation between these two men was like. When I think of Moses approaching the Egyptian king to ask for the release of the Hebrew people, I imagine him being very nervous and probably uncomfortable given that he was confronting the very man he had once served.

Moses' audacious request and Pharaoh's retort brought about a great conflict. Moses asked that the Hebrew people return to Canaan, where they were from, but Pharaoh insisted they remain in Egypt. He refused to let them go. Why would he? After all, these precious Hebrew slaves were vital to the flourishing economy.

Is response to Pharaoh's refusal, God declared a series of plagues on the people of Egypt. The ten plagues were especially awe-inspiring and shocking spectacles. After the ninth plague that God struck upon the Egyptian people, Pharaoh remained stubborn. He gave Moses a final threat. There was no more room for negotiating, and if Moses came back to the palace he would be killed. "Pharaoh said to Moses, 'Get out of my sight! Make sure you do not appear before me again! The day you see my face you will die.' 'Just as you say,' Moses replied. 'I will never appear before you again'"(Exodus 10:28-29).

Then Moses declared God's tenth plague, the death of the firstborn. Moses said, "Every firstborn son in Egypt will die, from the firstborn son of Pharaoh, who sits on the throne, to the firstborn son of the female slave, who is at her hand mill, and all the firstborn of the cattle as well. There will be loud wailing throughout Egypt - worse than there has ever been or ever will be again"(Exodus 11:5-6).

Pandemonium erupted. In the middle of the night, the Egyptian people woke up to face the tragedy. The firstborn of every household and of all livestock in Egypt was killed. Even Pharaoh's firstborn son was killed. The Hebrew people, however, were exempt from God's order of death, as they had marked the doors of their houses with blood and were protected as God's people.

When a loved one in a family dies, their household needs time to grieve. Life continues on in a normal fashion for those not personally affected by the loss, but for the surviving family and friends, it seems as if their world stops. Appointments are cancelled, days are taken off from work or school, and other obligations are put aside for a time. Not to mention the excruciating heartbreak and suffering that is endured emotionally. Now imagine a community where one person in every household passes away in the same night. Imagine the insanity. It's hard to even think about, isn't it? Well, that's what happened in Egypt on the night of the tenth plague. People were beside themselves. The entire country was in chaos. Life was no longer the same for every single family in that part of the world.

The plague was so devastating that Pharaoh finally gave in to Moses' demands. He sent for Moses and his brother Aaron in the early hours of the morning and told them, "Up! Leave my people, you and the Israelites! Go, worship the LORD as you have requested. Take your flocks and herds, as you have said, and go. And also bless me"(Exodus 12:31-32).

Four hundred and thirty years after the Israelites first arrived in Egypt, they finally were able to return to their homeland. Numbers 1:46 tells us that there were six hundred thousand able-bodied men over the age of twenty alone that made up this group of Hebrews. The tradition at that time was to only count in the census males between the ages of twenty and sixty who were able to fight in battle. The total population of the Exodus, therefore, including all men, women, and children can be estimated at around 2.5 million. It was an extraordinary event.

The Passover is the Jewish holiday that commemorates the Exodus. It's important to note that this "holiday" began in Egypt and afterward was celebrated and observed as the first of three feasts of the Jews. At the last supper Jesus observed the Passover, and when He was crucified, He became the lamb of the last Passover.

The Collapse of Egyptian Empire

Following the command of God, Moses did not lead the people through the land of the Philistines, even though it would have been the most direct route. Instead, he took them the way of the Red Sea. God knew the Hebrews might consider giving up and returning to Egypt if they had to fight, so He purposely directed them on a one-way-only path(see Exodus 13:17-18).

From the moment they took the first step of their journey toward the Promised Land, God began to unleash His supernatural power. He performed miracles throughout the voyage. The first was giving them a pillar of cloud to lead them on their way. "By day the LORD went ahead of them in a pillar of cloud to guide them on their way and by night in a pillar of fire to give them light, so that they could travel by day or night. Neither the pillar of cloud by day nor the pillar of fire by night left its place in front of the people"(Exodus 13:21-22).

The second miracle came in the form of the Red Sea. Some time after the Hebrew people left Egypt, Pharaoh began to regret his decision. He wanted his slaves back. "So he had his chariot made ready and took his army with him. He took six hundred of the best chariots, along with all the other chariots of Egypt, with officers over all of them. The LORD hardened the

The Crossing of the Red Sea
by Cosimo Rosselli

heart of Pharaoh king of Egypt, so that he pursued the Israelites, who were marching out boldly. The Egyptians - all Pharaoh's horses and chariots, horsemen and troops - pursued the Israelites and overtook them as they camped by the sea near Pi Hahiroth, opposite Baal Zephon"(Exodus 14:6-9).

When this happened, Israel panicked. They saw the Red Sea in front of them and the Egyptian army behind them. They were sandwiched in between two enemies. Although the people started worrying and complaining - something they had a habit of doing the entire time in the desert - God was preparing another miracle. When he heard their grumbling, Moses encouraged them.

> "Moses answered the people, "Do not be afraid. Stand firm and you will see the deliverance the LORD will bring you today. The Egyptians you see today you will never see again. The LORD will fight for you; you need only to be still." Then the LORD said to Moses, "Why are you crying out to me? Tell the Israelites to move on. Raise your staff and stretch out your hand over the sea to divide the water so that the Israelites can go through the sea

on dry ground"(Exodus 14:13-16).

I don't know what the Hebrews were thinking at that moment. I'm sure some believed Moses and others doubted. Maybe some thought the whole thing was plain crazy. But just as He said, God parted the waters of the Red Sea and the people of Israel walked right through the sea on dry land. As they walked, the Egyptian army followed close behind ready to capture and once again enslave them.

> "During the last watch of the night the LORD looked down from the pillar of fire and cloud at the Egyptian army and threw it into confusion. He jammed the wheels of their chariots so that they had difficulty driving. And the Egyptians said, 'Let's get away from the Israelites! The LORD is fighting for them against Egypt'"(Exodus 14:24-25).

God ordered Moses to stretch his hand out over the fleeing Egyptians. He resumed the natural flow of the Red Sea, thereby drowning the entire army, every soldier and every chariot. (The modern day equivalent of a chariot is a fighter jet. A loss of one jet is devastating to an army. Imagine the loss of a country's entire fleet of fighter jets.) Not only was this a shocking and demoralizing loss to Egypt, it also helped drown their dream of becoming an empire.

The Hebrew people now had the opportunity to start a new life of freedom. I am fascinated by the fact that they studied the law of Moses with such devotion during their journey into the Promised Land. Through their commitment to keep learning the law, they became one of the cleverest people in the world.

The Reign of King Solomon

I want to jump ahead to the future and talk about the relationship between the Egypt and the Israel of King Solomon's era, five hundred years after the Hebrews entered the land of Canaan.

"Solomon made an alliance with Pharaoh king of Egypt and married his daughter. He brought her to the City of David until he finished building his palace and the temple of the LORD, and the wall around Jerusalem" (1 King 3:1). The king of a country that had once enslaved and ruled over the Hebrews was put in a position where he had to marry his daughter off to that very nation for political reasons. (His daughter did not marry Solomon as the only queen but as one of a thousand concubines.) The dramatic shift in the relationship between these two nations is obvious.

Five hundred years drastically changed the political climate of the Near East. Egypt had lost more than one million free laborers and had all of her military power obliterated; therefore, she was no longer a force with which to be reckoned. The nation of Israel, on the other hand, was powerful and wealthy. During the time of Solomon's rule, Israel had 1,400 chariots and 12,000 horsemen. The king actually imported horses and chariots from Egypt(see 1 Kings 10:27-29). Notice the irony. King Solomon, who was known in the Bible as the wisest man who ever lived, amassed great wealth during his reign. First Kings 10:16-17 tells us that Solomon

King Solomon and Queen Sheba
by Konrad Bitch

had two hundred shields made of pure gold that were carried by guards throughout his palace.

When King Solomon died, his forty-one-year-old son Rehoboam ascended to the throne. It was during this time that the nation of Israel was divided in half by two kingdoms, the Northern Kingdom of Israel (not to be confused with Israel, the united nation) and Judah in the south. King Rehoboam ruled over Judah. This division brought about the decline of the Hebrew nation's power.

The kingdom of Judah departed from God and began to serve other idols and live a life of sin. "Judah did evil in the eyes of the LORD. By the sins they committed they stirred up his jealous anger more than those who were before them had done. They also set up for themselves high places, sacred stones and Asherah poles on every high hill and under every spreading tree"(1 Kings 14:22-23).

Consequently, Judah became unable to defend herself against Egypt, who had managed to rebuild her military, although not to its former glory. In the fifth year of King Rehoboam's reign, the Egyptian King Shisak invaded Jerusalem and took away treasures of the temple and the palace, including the gold shields of Solomon I mentioned above(see 1 Kings 14:25-27).

The eras of Kings David and Solomon's reign are prime examples of how willing and able God is to bless those who whole-heartedly serve Him. The reign of Rehoboam, however, is evidence of the trouble that comes when one turns away from the ways of the Lord. As mentioned in Leviticus 26:8, the book that contains the laws of the kingdom of priests, if people keep the law of God, five people can defeat a hundred and one hundred can defeat ten thousand. It's simple - if people follow God, He will protect them (the best kind of national defense). If people do not follow God's ways, however, He will not come to their rescue.

King Josiah and the Fate of Egypt

After the division of Israel, a total of twenty kings ruled Judah. There were good and bad kings in the mix. One of the good kings was Josiah, who reigned over Judah. He was loved by the people and followed after God. "He did what was right in the eyes of the LORD and followed completely the ways of his father David, not turning aside to the right or to the left"(2 Kings 22:2).

One thing he did that pleased God was to reestablish the observance of the Passover, which the nation of Israel had not been honoring. "The king gave this order to all the people: 'Celebrate the Passover to the LORD your God, as it is written in this Book of the Covenant.' Neither in the days of the judges who led Israel nor in the days of the kings of Israel and the kings of Judah had any such Passover been observed. But in the eighteenth year of King Josiah, this Passover was celebrated to the LORD in Jerusalem"(2 Kings 23:21-23).

During King Josiah's reign, a lot of changes were happening on an international level. Power was shifting among the great empires, as were loyalties. The long-feared Assyrian empire was coming to an end as its biggest enemies Babylon, Scythe, and Media united in power against her and moved to invade the Assyrian city of Nineveh. This proved to be a pivotal turn of events for King Josiah.

Kneeling Statue of Necho II
by Unknown Artist

Knowing her enemies were plotting to invade, Assyria approached King Necho (or Pharaoh, as the Egyptian kings were known) of Egypt for help. As the Egyptian army began its march to join forces with Assyria, King Josiah, hoping to gain favor with the Babylonian king, met the Egyptian forces before they were able to join Assyria. The battle took place in Megiddo, where most of Israel's battles occurred, and resulted in the death of the Judean king and the Egyptians gaining control of Judah.

> "While Josiah was king, Pharaoh Necho king of Egypt went up to the Euphrates River to help the king of Assyria. King Josiah marched out to meet him in battle, but Necho faced him and killed him at Megiddo. Josiah's servants brought his body in a chariot from Megiddo to Jerusalem and buried him in his own tomb. And the people of the land took Jehoahaz son of Josiah and anointed him and made him king in place of his father" (2 Kings 23:29-30).

After the battle of Megiddo, Egypt forged forward with a weakened army and joined the fight with Assyria to overtake the Babylonians. Egypt and Assyria were unsuccessful, and the Egyptian army retreated. Necho took captive King Jehoahaz of Judah, who was only in power for three months. Pharaoh then made Josiah's son Eliakim the new king and changed his name to Jehoiakim(see 2 Kings 23:34). As payment for being enthroned as king, Necho demanded King Jehoiakim pay tribute to Egypt. The Judean king obliged and taxed the people of Israel to come up with the payment(see 2 Kings 23:35).

Babylon continued to acquire considerable strength and power in the ancient Near East and posed a viable threat to Egypt. The two countries were at odds with each other, and the conflict put King Jehoiakim in an awkward situation. While he was paying tribute to Egypt who had made him king, he couldn't ignore the reckoning force of Babylon. So the king of Judah switched his alliance and joined with Babylon. The coupling didn't last long, however, and after three years, Judah rejoined forces with Egypt.

The Downfall of Egypt

In the fourth year of King Jehoiakim's rule, Babylon, led by King Nebuchadnezzar, marched out to strike Egypt in the historical battle of Carchemish, which was near the Euphrates River(see Jeremiah 46:2).

Historian Flavius Josephus recorded that King Necho advanced to the city of Carchemish prepared to fight to the death. Babylon took the enemy's intentions seriously and brought to battle its great army. When the battle was over, several hundred thousand Egyptian soldiers were killed, marking another great defeat since the Exodus.[6)] This second devastation was the final straw that forever ended Egypt's dream of becoming an empire. She was totally defeated in this battle, and Babylon accumulated a significant amount of territory to expand its empire(see 2 Kings 24:7).

Considered a part of the "cradle of civilization," Egypt was not beyond being destroyed. The prophet Isaiah foretold of her destruction.

> "A prophecy against Egypt: See, the LORD rides on a swift cloud and is coming to Egypt. The idols of Egypt tremble before him, and the hearts of the Egyptians melt with fear. 'I will stir up Egyptian against Egyptian - brother will fight against brother, neighbor against neighbor, city against city, kingdom against kingdom. The Egyptians will lose heart, and I will bring their plans to nothing; they will consult the idols and the spirits of the dead, the mediums and the spiritists. I will hand the Egyptians

over to the power of a cruel master, and a fierce king will rule over them,' declares the Lord, the LORD Almighty"(Isaiah 19:1-4).

The grand defeat of Egypt and the continued fighting between powerful forces like Assyria and Babylon left the nation of Israel in a vulnerable position, especially because of her geographical location, and required the kings to mobilize their political power with allies of other nations to maintain diplomacy and protect their kingdoms.

God, however, knew that it was more important to depend on Him than in strong and powerful forces, whether armies, countries, or empires. He sent prophets to the nation of Israel to remind them that keeping the laws of God is the key to solving political problems, keeping peace, and protecting their country.

Judah did not heed God's warning as sent through the prophet Isaiah. They feared the possibility of being destroyed by a powerful country. As a matter of fact, that fear was greater than their fear of God. As time would tell, however, Egypt would be conquered by Babylon and eventually by the empires of Persia, Greece, and Rome.

God's Management of the Universe

I like to think that Mother Nature, unleashed by the hand of God, had a lot to do with the way Egypt ascended to power. At the beginning of their civilization, the Egyptians developed their agriculture economy by utilizing the natural, fertile conditions of the Nile. When the seven years of abundance and seven years of famine were foretold through Pharaoh's dream, Joseph was quickly ushered into power to oversee those coming times. He was even given the daughter of an Egyptian priest to marry so he could have authority to rule over the nation. No matter what the turn of events, it was God, not Pharaoh, who put Joseph into the second most powerful seat in the Egyptian government.

While Joseph excelled at governing the kingdom during both the time of abundance and famine, we must remember it was God who caused the land to flourish and subsequently dry up. It's important to note that it was also God's will for the Hebrew nation to enter Egypt through means of the famine. The lesson here, and in all things, is that God is in charge. Although farmers can work hard from dawn until dusk, planting seeds using their great knowledge and the most advanced equipment available, they cannot expect to harvest if God does not provide the necessary sunlight and rain. No matter how abundant a nation, famine just may be around the corner. It was not by Egypt's outstanding skills that she enjoyed a prosperous run; it was only by the grace of God.

When the Hebrew people grew in number, Egypt had to face the reality that she could not expand into an empire. Threatened, Egypt took cruel and drastic action. It took the God-ordained leading of Moses, a baby born in secret during the time when boys were ordered to be killed, to flee and settle into the Promised Land. Egypt's calculated intentions and drastic efforts to grow into a powerful empire could not help but submit to the Providence of nature as led by God. A prosperous country is no match for Mother Nature. This is because she was created by and belongs to God, not manufactured or to be used by man.

The Rise and Fall of the 5 Empires in the Bible

CHAPTER 1
BIBLE with ASSYRIAN EMPIRE

The Bible books related to Assyria

Jonah, Nahum, Isaiah, Amos,
II Kings, II Chronicles etc.

Assyria, the Master of Asia for 520 Years

Arnold C. Brackman wrote in *The Luck of Nineveh* that, even though the Assyrian Empire had the longest run of all empires, by the time the famous archeologist Austen Henry Layard was born in 1817, there was no evidence that Nineveh, the capital of Assyria, ever existed.

In the early nineteenth century, before any trace of Nineveh was discovered, many skeptics, influenced by the scientific developments of the time, considered the story of Assyria a joke.[7)] Their religious faith in Biblical teachings wavered. They needed archeological ruins or some hard evidence to prove the empire ever existed. But the Bible confirms Assyria did, in fact, exist. And despite the advances in science and technology that seem to challenge Biblical history, especially during the Industrial Revolution, the Word as inspired by God is not to be disbelieved. Anyone who thinks otherwise is probably too proud or foolish to accept the Word of God.

The Greek historian Herodotus, whom Cicero dubbed the "father of history," gave us some background into the ancient civilization, thereby proving Assyria's existence. In his record of the battle between Persia and Greece (449-450 BC), he wrote, "The Assyrians had been masters of upper Asia over a period of five hundred and twenty years, when the Medes set the example of revolt from their authority."[8]

Herodotus also wrote about the makeup and quality of the Assyrian land. "The rainfall of Assyria is slight and provides enough moisture only to burst the seed and start the root growing, but to swell the grain and bring it to maturity artificial irrigation is used, not, as in Egypt, by the natural flooding of the river, but by hand-worked swipes. Like Egypt, the whole country is intersected by dykes; the largest of them has to be crossed in boats and runs in a south-easterly direction from the Euphrates until it joins another river, the Tigris, on which Nineveh was built."[9]

About the time when skepticism had reached its peak, British archeologist Austen Henry Layard discovered ruins of Nineveh in 1847. His findings put all doubts to rest and brought Assyria to light. (Layard's discoveries were eventually moved to England and put on display at the British Museum.)

Layard endured a lot of challenges during the beginning of his excavation and spent more than a year searching for ruins until he made his discovery in the mounds of Mesopotamia. After many setbacks, he realized the best way to excavate these mounds. In building their temples, the Assyrians laid down a platform of sun-dried bricks about nine or ten meters above sea level. Over time, the accumulation of windblown sand and dust covered the ruins that lay over the platforms. These piles looked like little hills. Layard realized that he must first search for these platforms. Once he found the

Sir Austen H. Layard (1817-1894)
by Author Anonymous

platform, he needed to dig a trench down to its level and no deeper. After a few days of digging, he found a platform about six meters down from the top of the mound.[10]

In continuing his excavation, Layard went on to unearth the city wall that surrounded Nineveh. The length of the wall was thirteen kilometers, and the height reached more than sixty meters above the ground. The thickness of the wall was about the width of three carriages. Nineveh was protected by five walls in total and three outer lakes, which served to protect the more than thirty temples made of gold and silver throughout the city.[11]

Here's an interesting fact about the ancient city of Nineveh: According to one historical record, eventually the whole city of Nineveh was covered by the flood waters of the Tigris River, and dirt and sand were piled as high as twenty feet, or six meters, over the temples.[12] This event would fulfill the prophecy as told in the book of Nahum.

It's also interesting to note that, about two hundred years after the Assyrian Empire was destroyed in battle, ten thousand Greek soldiers passed through this area en route to conquer Persia. They had no idea that Nineveh, the very seat of Assyria's infamous power, was lying right under their feet.[13]

Assyria started out as a small country, claiming territory about one hundred and sixty kilometers wide and six hundred and forty kilometers long. But she increased her imperial rule and conquered Asia Minor, which stretched as far as India in the east, Egypt in the west, Russia to the north, and even Arabian Felix in the south. Eventually her territory stretched about thirty-two hundred kilometers long from grassland to desert.[14] This tremendous empire disappeared without a trace and was rediscovered more than two thousand years later with the help of archeology.

Layard's methods influenced future archeologists. A century later, German archeologist Heinrich Schliemann publicly said, "I learned a lot from Layard, [to] whom I owe a debt."[15] It was Schliemann who discovered the remains of Troy and became known as the "father of archeology."

The British Museum and the Remains of Assyria

A lot of countries have wonderful museums, but in my opinion the Louvre in France and the British Museum in England have the most historical treasures. I visited the British Museum many times during my eight years of study in England. It was my favorite attraction. The museum houses more than two million pieces of invaluable historical artifacts.

The museum, which, unbelievably, is free of charge, is more than just a beautiful building showing important artifacts from past civilizations and countries around the world. The staff invests a great deal of time, effort, and money to create and showcase their exhibits. They are passionate about what they do and strive to help visitors think about history in a real and meaningful way. I boast of the museum so much, sometimes I feel like I'm on their public relations committee!

While I love visiting the museum with guests, I especially enjoy exploring it on my own. One day I went to study the exhibits more thor-

The British Museum

oughly than I ever had and discovered a wonderful thing. I passed through the museum entrance and carefully surveyed the displayed artifacts beginning near the left door. I found that the artifacts were shown in the order of empires mentioned in the Bible — Assyria, Babylon, Persia, Greece, and Rome. I was drawn to the fact that the Assyrian artifacts, as many as 1,106, were exactly the same as mentioned in the Bible. (Unfortunately, those ancient objects are no longer on display and can only be viewed online.)

My younger daughter majored in archeology at University College London (UCL). On occasion, she visits the Department of Conservation and Science at the British Museum to study the artifacts that are not yet ready to be shown. According to her, the artifacts stored in the underground room are quite remarkable. She explained the complicated and thorough process that each artifact undergoes to verify its value and meaning. This is a process that I deeply respect and am fascinated by. (I am told that a lot of Assyrian artifacts are also displayed in the Louvre; perhaps one day I will visit that famous museum.)

Even though the discovery of Assyrian artifacts served to verify its existence, it does not mean the Bible alone is insufficient evidence to substantiate ancient history. I believe the Bible to be truth, not a myth or an ancient story. It's important to study the text in order to understand the

Louvre Museum

past. Most records about Assyria can be found in the Bible. The book of Nahum includes prophecies about it, and the book of Jonah talks about God's judgment and forgiveness for the people of Nineveh. If scholars and laypeople alike want to learn about empires, this remarkable one in particular, they should study the Bible.

Generally speaking, we can't move forward into the future until we look backward. The Bible tells us a lot about God's views and management of the world in the past, the present, and future. When we study both the Bible and the ancient artifacts like those found in the British Museum, we have more than enough evidence to learn about history and even catch a glimpse into the future.

The Prophet Jonah

Many people think of the prophet Jonah as the man who disobeyed God. But there is more to the story than this man's rebellion. He had a repentant heart. God loved him and recognized him as a prophet. (I wish there was a statement at the end of the book of Jonah that highlights how this prophet repented and followed the call of God.)

The short, four-chapter book of Jonah is a love story of how God loves not just "chosen people" but all people. When God called the prophet, Jonah's country, the Northern Kingdom of Israel, was lost in idolatry and evil. At the same time, Assyria was building and growing her tremendous empire through imperialism and, as a result, striking fear in the hearts of surrounding countries.

In the mid to late 700s BC, God told Jonah to go to Assyria and proclaim the plan of salvation by declaring judgment on the people of Nineveh. "Go to the great city of Nineveh and preach against it, because its

Stone Tablet from Nineveh's Sennacherib Palace _ The British Museum

wickedness has come up before me"(Jonah 1:2). Nineveh was the last place Jonah wanted to be, so at first he didn't obey God's call. I imagine Jonah was upset because God told him to go to the enemy, not to his own people. Whatever he thought, Jonah fled and, instead of heading to Nineveh, he boarded a ship from Joppa that would take him to the city of Tarshish.

Most of us know the story well. There was a great storm and the passengers on the ship decided Jonah was bad luck and threw him overboard. The storm ceased and a great fish, sent by God, swallowed Jonah. In the belly of the fish Jonah prayed to God, and God spoke to him a second time giving him the same mission. "Go to the great city of Nineveh and proclaim to it the message I give you"(Jonah 3:2). The prophet finally obeyed.

According to Jonah's account, Nineveh was so big that it would take him three days to walk through the city so everyone could hear the message that God would destroy Nineveh in forty days(see Jonah 3:4). But the prophet was such a naturally talented speaker and the news spread unbelievably fast, that after only a day of traveling, the entire city had heard the Word of the Lord.

It seems God chose the right man for the job; He knew what He was doing when He sent Jonah as His prophet. God has a habit of using all sorts of people with different backgrounds and even questionable attitudes, like

Jonah Preaches in Nineveh
by Gustave Dore

Jonah, to further His kingdom. For instance, God used Paul, the persecutor of Christians, to spread the gospel to Jews and Greeks alike.

Most people think the miracle in this book was that Jonah was swallowed alive by a fish and spat out after three days. But the real miracle was that the people of Nineveh, from servants to dignitaries, sat on ashes, repented, prayed, fasted, and believed in God. This is the wonderful message of God — anyone can be saved if they repent.

Even the king repented. "When Jonah's warning reached the king of Nineveh, he rose from his throne, took off his royal robes, covered himself with sackcloth and sat down in the dust. This is the proclamation he issued in Nineveh: "By the decree of the king and his nobles: Do not let people or animals, herds or flocks, taste anything; do not let them eat or drink. But let people and animals be covered with sackcloth. Let everyone call urgently on God. Let them give up their evil ways and their violence. Who knows? God may yet relent and with compassion turn from his fierce anger so that we will not perish"(Jonah 3:6-10).

Because the people of Nineveh repented, God did not bring about the destruction he had planned. God loves a repentant heart. It greatly pleases Him to forgive all people, no matter how evil they are or what bad things they have done. The book of First Kings tells us of the very powerful and very evil King Ahab of the Northern Kingdom of Israel. The prophet Elijah was sent by God to tell King Ahab that because he was so evil, God was going to kill him and his entire family.

Immediately, the king tore his clothes, girded his body with thick

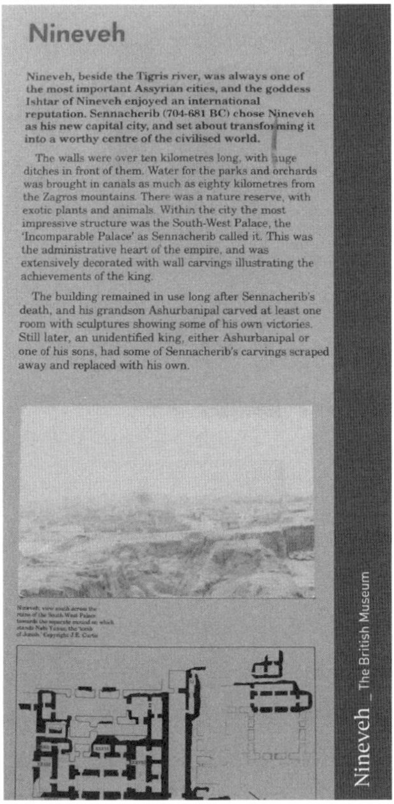

sackcloth, fasted, and went about his business deeply humbled. God was moved by his sincere repentance and told Elijah, "Have you noticed how Ahab has humbled himself before me? Because he has humbled himself, I will not bring this disaster in his day, but I will bring it on his house in the days of his son"(1 Kings 21:29).

At first I did not understand why God was so pleased with such a small act of repentance in spite of the great evil carried out by King Ahab. But eventually I began to understand the deep love of God and His willingness to forgive people. God was concerned with the people of Nineveh because they didn't have a moral compass; He thought they deserved another chance. God said, "And should I not have concern for the great city of Nineveh, in which there are more than a hundred and twenty thousand people who cannot tell their right hand from their left — and also many animals?"(Jonah 4:11).

The Assyrians who were saved through the preaching of Jonah(see Matthew 12:41) should have produced the kind of fruitful life that is marked by repentance. However, Assyria as a whole did not give up her ambition of imperialism and continued in her evil ways. One hundred and fifty years after Jonah was on the scene, the prophet Nahum alerted Assyria to the coming destruction of her empire.

The Northern Kingdom of Israel and Assyria

After Moses led Israel out of Egypt, the Hebrews wandered in the desert for forty years before they arrived in the Promised Land. For the next three hundred years, judges ruled the nation of Israel. This period was known as the Era of Judges and ended with the rule of the last judge, Samuel. Then began a monarchy that lasted five hundred years. Israel was a united nation for the first one hundred and twenty years under the rule of Kings Saul, David, and Solomon, each for forty years.

After the end of Solomon's reign, the nation split into two kingdoms, the Northern Kingdom of Israel and Judah in the south. The Northern Kingdom of Israel was eventually overtaken by Assyria. Judah enjoyed one hundred and fifty more years as a kingdom, but was eventually conquered by Babylon, who claimed the Hebrews as captives for seventy years. During the monarch of Judah, she was ruled by a total of twenty kings, most of whom were evil; only a few ruled in the way of King David, a man known for having a heart after God.

Assyria Relief of the Wing King from the City of Nimrud_ Metropolitan Museum of Art

The Biblical books of First and Second Kings and First and Second Chronicles record the histories of these two kingdoms. I'd like to talk about the relationship between the Northern Kingdom of Israel and Assyria as delineated in the books of Kings.

In a span of two hundred years, the Northern Kingdom of Israel went through seven coups (which shows just how violent her history was) and nineteen different kings (Jeroboam I, Nadab, Baasha, Elah, Jimri, Omri, Ahab, Ahaziah, Jehoram, Jehu, Jehoahaz, Jehoash, Jeroboam II, Zechariah, Shallum, Menahem, Pekahiah, Pekah, and Hoshea).

All nineteen kings were evil. They took after Jeroboam, the first and very wicked king. The Biblical examples below show the character of Kings Jehoahaz (the eleventh king), Jehoash (the twelfth king), and Jeroboam II (the thirteenth king).

> "In the twenty-third year of Joash son of Ahaziah king of Judah, Jehoahaz son of Jehu became king of Israel in Samaria, and he reigned seventeen years. He did evil in the eyes of the LORD by following the sins of Jeroboam son of Nebat, which he had caused Israel to commit, and he did not turn away from them" (2 Kings 13:1-2).

> "In the thirty-seventh year of Joash king of Judah, Jehoash son of Jehoahaz became king of Israel in Samaria, and he reigned sixteen years. He did evil in the eyes of the LORD and did not turn away from any of the sins of Jeroboam son of Nebat, which he had caused Israel to commit; he continued in them"(2 Kings 13:10-11).

> "In the fifteenth year of Amaziah son of Joash king of Judah, Jeroboam son of Jehoash king of Israel became king in Samaria, and he reigned forty-one years. He did evil in the eyes of the LORD and did not turn away from any of the sins of Jeroboam son of Nebat, which he had caused Israel to commit"(2 Kings 14:23-24).

Because the governing powers of the Northern Kingdom of Israel did not follow in the ways of God, they were always in a state of crisis and reg-

Stone Tablet from Tiglath-Pileser III's Palace_The British Museum

ularly plagued by civil unrest. Also, there were constant threats by the powerful empire of Assyria, who invaded her when King Menahem, the sixteenth king, was enthroned.

Menahem killed Salum, the king before him who had ruled only for one month, and reigned for ten years beginning in 752 BC. When Assyria invaded Israel, Menahem paid off the Assyrian king Tiglath-Pileser III so he could retain his throne. The Bible tells us that the Israeli king forced the rich to help pay for the thousand-talent bribe.

> "Then Pul king of Assyria invaded the land, and Menahem gave him a thousand talents of silver to gain his support and strengthen his own hold on the kingdom. Menahem exacted this money from Israel. Every wealthy person had to contribute fifty shekels of silver to be given to the king of Assyria. So the king of Assyria withdrew and stayed in the land no longer"(2 Kings 15:19-20).

The British historian Paul Johnson wrote about this very event in *A History of the Jews*. "Throughout the ninth century the power of Assyria had been growing. The Black Obelisk of Shalmaneser shows that, even in Jehu's day, Israel had been forced to pay tribute. For a time Israel bought the Assyrians off, or formed coalitions of other small states to halt their advance. But in 745 BC the cruel Tiglath-Pileser III ascended the Assyrian throne and turned his warlike race into a nation of imperialists. He inaugurated a policy of mass deportation in conquered territories. In 740 his annals record: 'As for Menahem [King of Israel] terror overwhelmed him... he fled and submitted to me... silver, coloured woollen garments, linen garments... I received as his tribute.' In 734 he broke through to the coast, then advanced down it to 'the Brook of Egypt'."

Tiglath-Pileser III was a soldier in the Assyrian army who usurped the throne in 745 BC and made Assyria the strongest country in the world. The Assyrian king, called Pul in the Bible, had a brutal desire for conquest and a vast knowledge of military strategy. He had dreamt of one day occupying Syria, Israel, and Egypt, using the latter country as his base. (The British Museum displays his remains.)

The Black Obelisk of Shalmaneser III
The British Museum

King Tiglath-Pileser III occupied the Northern Kingdom of Israel when Israel's King Pekah — who became the eighteenth king after he killed Pekaiah, the seventeenth king and Menahem's son — was in power. The Assyrian army began to deport the people of Israel to their country. "In the time of Pekah king of Israel, Tiglath-Pileser king of Assyria came and took Ijon, Abel Beth Maakah, Janoah, Kedesh and Hazor. He took Gilead and Galilee, including all the land of Naphtali, and deported the people to Assyria"(2 Kings 15:29).

King Pekah quickly joined an alliance with the country of Aram and proposed to Judah that they, too, become allies. Judah, however, thought it was better to maintain a friendly policy with Assyria and refused King Pekah's proposal. So Aram and the Northern Kingdom of Israel, whose strength by this time was nearly drained, began to make plans to invade Judah first before standing against Assyria. With this impending threat, King Ahaz of Judah urgently sent a messenger to King Tiglath-Pileser III and asked him for help.

> "'I am your servant and vassal. Come up and save me out of the hand of the king of Aram and of the king of Israel, who are attacking me.' And Ahaz took the silver and gold found in the temple of the LORD and in the treasuries of the royal palace and sent it as a gift to the king of Assyria. The king of Assyria complied by attacking Damascus and capturing it. He deported its inhabitants to Kir and put Rezin to death"(2 Kings 16:7-9).

I don't think King Ahaz envisioned that his letter would be published for the entire world to read. It's embarrassing and disgraceful for a king to say he is a "servant and vassal" to another country's king. It was custom, however, for countries that received these kinds of amusing messages to keep them as records.

In the Northern Kingdom of Israel, where violence had become a daily phenomenon, King Pekah was killed through yet another coup, and Hoshea—who sat on the throne beginning in 732 BC — became the nineteenth and last king of Israel. The kingdom was ultimately destroyed in 722 BC.

A Lamassu _ The British Museum

Israel and the Prophets Elijah, Elisha, Amos, and Hosea

Neither Judah nor the Northern Kingdom of Israel followed God most of the time, and God was not pleased. He sent a string of prophets to speak to His people about repenting for the errors of their ways. These messages are found in the prophetic books of the Old Testament.

Many people consider these particular books of the Bible difficult to read and to study. It's probably because the prophets are speaking the words of God directly from Him and preaching about the present and the future at the same time. Or maybe people are challenged simply because they have not invested enough time in studying them.

Some books can be read once and the reader will immediately understand the subject. But other books require deep study and reflection to gain an understanding into its significance. There is a great benefit when they're read multiple times. Perhaps it's a little more work to do, but well worth it. The books of the prophets were given to us by God to read, study, and understand. If they weren't, God would not have included them in the Bible.

The premise of the prophetic books of the Bible is that God loves people and wants those who have turned away from Him to return. It's inspiring to study these books knowing the prophets were specifically sent by God because of His great compassion and love for humanity.

It's a shame that the kings of the Northern Kingdom of Israel walked in the way of Jeroboam and not the way of David. King Omri, in particular, was so evil he made God angry.

> "In the thirty-first year of Asa king of Judah, Omri became king of Israel, and he reigned twelve years, six of them in Tirzah. He

> bought the hill of Samaria from Shemer for two talents of silver and built a city on the hill, calling it Samaria, after Shemer, the name of the former owner of the hill. But Omri did evil in the eyes of the LORD and sinned more than all those before him. He followed completely the ways of Jeroboam son of Nebat, committing the same sin Jeroboam had caused Israel to commit, so that they aroused the anger of the LORD, the God of Israel, by their worthless idols"(2 Kings 16:23-26).

God was so angry at how evil and disobedient the next king, Ahab, was that He sent the prophet Elijah to speak to the Northern Kingdom of Israel. And after Elijah died, God sent Elisha in his place.

At the time of King Ahab's rule (874-853 BC), Assyria was expanding her empire in violent ways. The Assyrian King Shalmaneser III was increasing his power beyond the Euphrates River and posed a threat to the Northern Kingdom of Israel. Israel combined forces with Hamat and Damascus and together they went to war and fought a large-scale battle in Assyria and Karkar. The allied forces won this battle, but they would not win the war.

The British Museum has on display a tombstone from the Balawart Palace on which an Assyrian had written that out of the three allied forces,

A Bronze Band from the Gates of the Palace of Shalmaneser III
Balawat (Ancient Imgur-Enlil), Northern Iraq Neo-Assyrian, 858-824 B.C. (The British Museum)

King Ahab supplied two thousand chariots and ten thousand troops. This statement speaks of the once-remarkable economic and military power of the Northern Kingdom of Israel. But King Ahab was not only prosperous; he was also corrupt. His wife, Jezebel, was no different. She built places of worship to the gods of Baal and Asherah and stood against the prophet Elijah, even attempting to kill him.

You can see why it must have been difficult for Elisha to step into Elijah's shoes. He asked his teacher for a double portion of his spiritual power[16] so that he could continue the work of God. Not because he was greedy, but because he needed all the help he could get to carry out God's work in an increasingly wicked time.

> Elijah said to Elisha, "Tell me, what can I do for you before I am taken from you?"
> "Let me inherit a double portion of your spirit," Elisha replied.
> "You have asked a difficult thing," Elijah said, "yet if you see me when I am taken from you, it will be yours — otherwise, it will not."
> As they were walking along and talking together, suddenly a chariot of fire and horses of fire appeared and separated the two of them, and Elijah went up to heaven in a whirlwind(2 Kings 2:9-11).

Even though Elijah and Elisha preached the Word of God, the Northern Kingdom of Israel would never turn away from her evil ways. Therefore, God sent another prophet, Amos, a shepherd from Tekoa. He arrived on the scene in eighth century BC along with the prophet Hosea. At the same time, God sent the prophets Isaiah and Micah to Judah. God's heart was full of pain for both kingdoms of the nation of Israel.

The prophetic book of Amos begins with, "The words of Amos, one of the shepherds of Tekoa—the vision he saw concerning Israel two years before the earthquake, when Uzziah was king of Judah and Jeroboam son of Jehoash was king of Israel"(Amos 1:1).

The Balawat Gates, A Bronze Band from the Palace Gates of Ashurnasirpal II _ The British Museum

Amos pointed out the evils of the Northern Kingdom of Israel and urged the people to repent. In those days, the financial prosperity of the kingdom was at its peak. The wealthy built separate villas to spend winter and summer away from heat and cold and ate the highest quality and most expensive beef from Bashan. They also stole the garments of the poor and would not return them even on cold nights (a sign of their cruel ways).

The whole country worshiped idols and hated the prophets and the message they brought to the kingdom. It was a matter of time before these prophets, who poured their entire lives into preaching the words of God, burned out. So God sent another prophet, Hosea, to the Northern Kingdom of Israel.

> "The word of the LORD that came to Hosea son of Beeri during the reigns of Uzziah, Jotham, Ahaz and Hezekiah, kings of Judah, and during the reign of Jeroboam son of Jehoash king of Israel"(Hosea 1:1).

The Resettlement Policy of Assyria

During the rule of King Hoshea, King Shalmaneser V of Assyria attacked Israel, so the Israeli king paid tribute to him to remain on the throne. After a while, King Hoshea stopped the payments, which he had been sending every year, and looked to King So of Egypt for help. When Shalmaneser found out about the betrayal, he besieged the city of Samaria for three years and completely destroyed the Northern Kingdom of Israel.

> "In the ninth year of Hosea, the king of Assyria captured Samaria and deported the Israelites to Assyria. He settled them in Halah, in Gozan on the Habor River and in the towns of the Medes" (2 Kings 17:6).

God spoke about the destruction through the prophet Hosea and made mention of the people's fickle behavior. "Israel's arrogance testifies against him, but despite all this he does not return to the LORD his God or search for him. Ephraim is like a dove, easily deceived and senseless — now calling to Egypt, now turning to Assyria"(Hosea 7:10-11). God calls the Northern Kingdom of Israel "Ephraim" because their first king was from the tribe of Ephraim.

Not only did Shalmaneser deport the people of Israel to various locations throughout the Assyrian empire, he also imported people of other conquered nations to live in Samaria. "The king of Assyria brought people from Babylon, Kuthah, Avva, Hamath and Sepharvaim and settled them in the towns of Samaria to replace the Israelites. They took over Samaria and lived in its towns"(2 Kings 17:24). This was part of the Assyrian resettlement policy. It made for a population of mixed nations which prevented uprisings or revolt by individual nations of people. These actions were carried out in the name of imperialism.

After Assyria destroyed the Northern Kingdom of Israel, she turned her efforts to conquer the kingdom of Judah.

Judah's International Relations Policy and Assyrian Imperialism

The kings of Judah were Rehoboam, Abijah, Asa, Jehoshaphat, Joho-ram, Ahaziah, Athaliah, Joash, Amasha, Azariah (Uzziah), Jotham, Ahaz, Hezekiah, Manasseh, Amon, Josiah, Jehoahaz, Jehoiakim (Elijakim), Je-hoiachin, and Zedekiah.

In eighth century BC, at the same time the Northern Kingdom of Is-rael was ruled by Kings Menahem, Pekahiah, Pekah, and Hoshea, Judah was ruled by Kings Ahaz and Hezekiah. The prophet Isaiah was sent to Judah at that time to spread the Word of God. The first half of the prophet's life was spent preaching to King Ahaz. During the second part of his life, he helped King Hezekiah deliver the kingdom of Judah out of the hands of Assyria. Isaiah poured everything he had into fulfilling God's call on his life. He also suffered greatly during his ministry.

King Ahaz spent sixteen years on the throne beginning in 742 BC and was the ruler who turned down the offer to join the allied armies of Israel and Aram. The prophet Isaiah repeatedly tried to convince the king to change his diplomatic policy and abandon his alliance with Assyria. There

Assyrian Soldiers
The British Museum

A Stone Panel from the North-West Palace of Ashurnasirpal II _ The British Museum

were three reasons behind Isaiah's request. First, so that Judah would not be involved in any way in the fall of the Northern Kingdom of Israel. Second, to avoid religion conflicts that might arise if Judah became closer with Assyria. Third, it would ultimately be detrimental to Judah since Assyria would always try to expand her empire through invasive means.

Despite Isaiah's persistent advice to turn to God instead of Assyria, King Ahaz refused to heed his warnings. The king of Judah was ignorant of the effects of imperialism that the Northern Kingdom of Israel had experienced. Isaiah continued to tell the king that God was using Assyrian imperialism for His divine purpose, but the king only despised Isaiah's meddling in the kingdom's international diplomatic policy. Isaiah even challenged King Ahaz to seek a sign from God to prove Isaiah was right, but the king didn't even bother asking God for one. Why should he ask for a sign when he didn't even have enough faith to believe in Him?

> Again the LORD spoke to Ahaz, "Ask the LORD your God for a sign, whether in the deepest depths or in the highest heights." But Ahaz said, "I will not ask; I will not put the LORD to the test." Then Isaiah said, "Hear now, you house of David! Is it not enough to try the patience of humans? Will you try the patience of my God also? Therefore the Lord himself will give you a sign: The virgin will conceive and give birth to a son, and will call him Immanuel"(Isaiah 7:10-14).

The people of Judah refused to listen to the repeated warnings of the prophets and did not return to God. Therefore He stopped offering them opportunity after opportunity to repent. It was during this time that the Northern Kingdom of Israel proposed the alliance with Aram and Judah to fight Assyria. Isaiah warned Judah not to contribute to the destruction of the Northern Kingdom of Israel, but King Ahaz didn't listen and formed an alliance with Assyria instead.

Judah paid a large tribute to Assyria to maintain diplomacy. "Ahaz took some of the things from the temple of the LORD and from the royal palace and from the officials and presented them to the king of Assyria, but that did not help him"(2 Chronicles 28:21).

Until he died, King Ahaz depended on the powerful country of Assyria instead of on God. He put in place idols all over the kingdom including Baal and Ashera. He hoped his son, Hezekiah, who would ascend the throne after his death, would continue that alliance. After the death of King Ahaz, Judah continued its rule for one hundred and fifty years and was eventually destroyed, not by Assyria, however, but by Babylon.

King Ahaz's Greatest Mistake

One of Ahaz's greatest mistakes was authoring the infamous, humiliating letter to the Assyrian king Tiglath-Pileser III and giving away the temple's treasures. The king made yet another mistake, more dangerous than mere embarrassment.

> "Then King Ahaz went to Damascus to meet Tiglath-Pileser king of Assyria. He saw an altar in Damascus and sent to Uriah the priest a sketch of the altar, with detailed plans for its construc-

tion. So Uriah the priest built an altar in accordance with all the plans that King Ahaz had sent from Damascus and finished it before King Ahaz returned. When the king came back from Damascus and saw the altar, he approached it and presented offerings on it. He offered up his burnt offering and grain offering, poured out his drink offering, and splashed the blood of his fellowship offerings against the altar. As for the bronze altar that stood before the LORD, he brought it from the front of the temple — from between the new altar and the temple of the LORD — and put it on the north side of the new altar. King Ahaz then gave these orders to Uriah the priest: "On the large new altar, offer the morning burnt offering and the evening grain offering, the king's burnt offering and his grain offering, and the burnt offering of all the people of the land, and their grain offering and their drink offering. Splash against this altar the blood of all the burnt offerings and sacrifices. But I will use the bronze altar for seeking guidance." And Uriah the priest did just as King Ahaz had ordered"(2 Kings 16:10-16).

Ahaz Worship Idols in the Temple
by C. P. Marillier

When Assyria had conquered the kingdoms of Israel and Aram, the people held a triumphal celebration and invited King Ahaz to join the festivities. The purpose of the celebratory event was to announce to the people the victory of war, show them plunders, and comfort the family of the dead soldiers and give them financial recompense. At that time they needed a

The Garden Party from the Ashurbanipal Palace
The British Museum

religious ritual to commemorate the dead soldiers.

The Romans followed a similar procession after a victory. The general would ride on a magnificent chariot drawn by four white horses through an elaborate and solemn parade, a sacrifice would be made to the gods, and the general would offer a wreath to the gods, which signified that he had no intention of becoming king. Afterwards, a great banquet would be held and all the citizens would celebrate.

King Ahaz was impressed by the Assyrian processional and desired to imitate the event in his own kingdom. When he returned home, he commanded the people to bring offerings to sacrifice to the Assyrian god every day. I imagine the prophet Isaiah must have been sick as he witnessed this idolatrous spectacle.

The king didn't stop there. He also rearranged other items in the temple so it would be more pleasing to the Assyrian king. "King Ahaz cut off the side panels and removed the basins from the movable stands. He removed the Sea from the bronze bulls that supported it and set it on a stone base. He took away the Sabbath canopy that had been built at the temple and removed the royal entryway outside the temple of the LORD, in deference to the king of Assyria"(2 Kings 16:17-18). In essence, the king was saying he wanted to please Assyria more than he wanted to please God.

In the book of Leviticus, we see specific guidelines for sacrifice, given by God, which were to be used by His people. King Ahaz ignored these rules, his most grave refusal of God's ways, and maintained his dependence on Assyria instead of God until the day he died. The prophet Isaiah still had hope, however, and began to preach the Word to the king's son, Hezekiah.

Isaiah and Hezekiah Duel Over the National Security Policy

The meaning of the name Isaiah is "the Lord is salvation," which was the theme of the prophet's ministry. Isaiah's message was that God is the author of salvation, not powerful countries like Assyria. He took his job very seriously and even prophesied, according to God's command, naked for three years. "At that time the LORD spoke through Isaiah son of Amoz. He said to him, "Take off the sackcloth from your body and the sandals from your feet." And he did so, going around stripped and barefoot. Then the LORD said, "Just as my servant Isaiah has gone stripped and barefoot for three years, as a sign and portent against Egypt and Cush..."(Isaiah 20:2-3). The display of nudity was to show what great shame the people would suffer if they did not return to God.

The Prophet Isaiah _by Raffaello Sanzio da Urbino

A prophet's life wasn't easy. It was taxing on the heart, as evidenced by the prophet Jeremiah who preached the Word weeping so much his eyes were wounded by the tears. Also, sharing the message of God was not easy as much of the prophecies had to do with judgment and condemnation. Not only that, there were times God commanded the prophets to do strange things. Besides telling Isaiah to preach naked, God told the prophet Hosea to marry a prostitute. You can imagine how being a prophet led to living a very unpopular and hard life.

While Isaiah was committed to prophesying in Judah, and Assyria was expanding her empire through imperialism, a new force was on the horizon. Babylon was increasing in power and strength, quickly rising to become Assyria's biggest threat. In the middle of all this, Egypt was trying very hard to recover.

Isaiah primarily focused his efforts on King Hezekiah, but he did not concentrate his messages from God only on Israel. God used him to prophecy about other countries such as Assyria, Moab, and Damascus. The greatest prophecies were about the coming Messiah and directed to all mankind. All of his prophecies are contained in the sixty-six chapters of the Biblical book of Isaiah.

Hezekiah became king of Judah at the age of twenty-five. During the first half of the king's reign, he focused on national defense and formed an alliance with Egypt against Assyria. Isaiah criticized this political move and asked Hezekiah to shift his focus toward keeping God's laws and regulations, such as caring for the poor, instead of protecting his kingdom. Isaiah also asked the king to abandon the alliance with Egypt and rely only on God, not on the power of another country. Hezekiah, however, failed to accept Isaiah's advice and sided with Egypt.

Assyria was dismayed that King Hezekiah did not follow in the footsteps of his father to continue the alliance with the great empire. Assyria became angry at Judah's betrayal and launched an attack against her. A few years after Hezekiah became king, Assyria, ruled by King Sennacherib at the time, invaded Judah and began to occupy town after town, even threatening to attack Jerusalem.

The Biblical books of 2 Kings, 2 Chronicles, and Isaiah 36 detail Assyria's invasion of Judah. Second Kings tells us that King Sennacherib attacked and captured all of the cities of Judah. At this defeat, Hezekiah sent a message to the Assyrian king to relay his apologetic sentiments, just as his father had done before. He also paid him a considerable tribute.

> "In the fourteenth year of King Hezekiah's reign, Sennacherib king of Assyria attacked all the fortified cities of Judah and captured them. So Hezekiah king of Judah sent this message to the king of Assyria at Lachish: 'I have done wrong. Withdraw from me, and I will pay whatever you demand of me.' The king of Assyria exacted from Hezekiah king of Judah three hundred talents of silver and thirty talents of gold. So Hezekiah gave him all the silver that was found in the temple of the LORD and in the treasuries of the royal palace. At this time Hezekiah king of Judah stripped off the gold with which he had covered the doors and doorposts of the temple of the LORD, and gave it to the king of Assyria"(2 Kings 18:13-16).

The state of Judah's economy at that time was quite pitiful. Hezekiah did not even have the thirty talents of gold that was demanded of him by King Sennacherib. He actually had to strip the gold off the temple to come up with that tribute. How embarrassing!

This was a considerable difference compared to the state of the economy when Kings David and Solomon ruled the unified nation of Israel. I want to share with you some passages from the Bible that speak of the wealth that surrounded the initial vision and construction of the temple in their time.

King David conferred with his son Solomon and prepared one million talents of silver and one hundred thousand talents of gold for the construction of the temple. He even asked his son to prepare more to give as an offering. David said, "I have taken great pains to provide for the temple of the LORD a hundred thousand talents of gold, a million talents of silver, quantities of bronze and iron too great to be weighed, and wood and stone. And you may add to them. You have many workers: stonecutters, masons and carpenters, as well as those skilled in every kind of work in gold and silver, bronze and iron—craftsmen beyond number. Now begin the work, and the Lord be with you"(1 Chronicle 22:14-16).

David didn't stop there. Out of his deep commitment to building a house for the Lord, he gave an additional offering. The members of the king's inner circle respected this act of giving and contributed funds as well.

> "Besides, in my devotion to the temple of my God I now give my personal treasures of gold and silver for the temple of my God, over and above everything I have provided for this holy temple: three thousand talents of gold (gold of Ophir) and seven thousand talents of refined silver, for the overlaying of the walls of the buildings, for the gold work and the silver work, and for all the work to be done by the craftsmen. Now, who is willing to consecrate themselves to the LORD today?" Then the leaders of families, the officers of the tribes of Israel, the commanders of thousands and commanders of hundreds, and the officials in charge of the king's work gave willingly. They gave toward the work on the temple of God five thousand talents and ten thousand darics of gold, ten thousand talents of silver, eighteen thousand talents of bronze and a hundred thousand talents of iron (1 Chronicles 29:3-7).

The following Scripture references give us a glimpse of how much gold Solomon used to build this elaborate temple.

> "Solomon covered the inside of the temple with pure gold, and he

> extended gold chains across the front of the inner sanctuary, which was overlaid with gold. So he overlaid the whole interior with gold. He also overlaid with gold the altar that belonged to the inner sanctuary"(1 Kings 6:21-22).

> "Solomon also made all the furnishings that were in the LORD's temple: the golden altar, the golden table on which was the bread of the Presence; the lampstands of pure gold (five on the right and five on the left, in front of the inner sanctuary); the gold floral work and lamps and tongs; the pure gold basins, wick trimmers, sprinkling bowls, dishes and censers; and the gold sockets for the doors of the innermost room, the Most Holy Place, and also for the doors of the main hall of the temple. When all the work King Solomon had done for the temple of the LORD was finished, he brought in the things his father David had dedicated — the silver and gold and the furnishings — and he placed them in the treasuries of the LORD's temple"(1 Kings 7:48-51).

In reading the verses above, just imagine how much gold and silver Israel had accumulated over the years (and how much was taken away by having to pay all those tributes).

Second Chronicles tells us how after King Sennacherib threatened to destroy Jerusalem, King Hezekiah started a construction project to block all the sources of water outside Jerusalem to prevent the Assyrians from having access to water. Then brave soldiers from the army and the men of the kingdom joined together and defended Judah.

> "When Hezekiah saw that Sennacherib had come and that he intended to wage war against Jerusalem, he consulted with his officials and military staff about blocking off the water from the

> springs outside the city, and they helped him. They gathered a large group of people who blocked all the springs and the stream that flowed through the land. 'Why should the kings of Assyria come and find plenty of water?' they said. Then he worked hard repairing all the broken sections of the wall and building towers on it. He built another wall outside that one and reinforced the terraces of the City of David. He also made large numbers of weapons and shields." (2 Chronicles 32:2-5)

According to historian Paul Johnson, Hezekiah's plan received support from Am ha-aretz (the people of the land).[17] This was important because this was a top-secret construction project and it was necessary to garner approval from people of lower class. King Hezekiah opened the Siloam tunnel, brought in the stream water of Kihon to the water storage within the city, and made a waterway, allowing extra water to flow into Kidron stream. Should the Assyrian army siege the city, the people of Judah would have enough water to support their defense, and the Assyrians would be without. Archaeologist Kathleen Kenyon found this tunnel and proved its existence during her 1867-1870 excavation; according to her, the water flowed for as long as 1,200 cubits, or 1,749 feet.[18]

The Stupidity of the Genius Linguist

King Sennacherib, not satisfied with the payments from King Hezekiah, ordered his field commander to lead a great army from Lachish to fight against King Hezekiah. The commander stopped at the aqueduct of the Upper Pool and relayed to the palace administrator, recorder, and secretary the intentions of King Sennacherib(see Isaiah 36:1-3; the entire event is also told in 2 Kings 18:17-37 and 19).

The field commander spoke several languages fluently. He was able to speak his native tongue, Aramaic, as well as Hebrew, the Jewish language. He communicated the king's message in Hebrew, and did so very loudly. He wanted not only the government officials to hear what he was saying, but also the people of Judah who were near the palace walls. King Hezekiah's officials didn't want the people to understand the Assyrians threats, so they asked the field commander to speak in Aramaic. He refused, however, and said he wanted everyone in Judah to hear the message that they were all doomed to drink and eat his urine and excrement.

> Then the commander stood and called out in Hebrew, "Hear the words of the great king, the king of Assyria! This is what the king says: Do not let Hezekiah deceive you. He cannot deliver you! Do not let Hezekiah persuade you to trust in the LORD when he says, 'The LORD will surely deliver us; this city will not be given into the hand of the king of Assyria.'
> "Do not listen to Hezekiah. This is what the king of Assyria says: Make peace with me and come out to me. Then each of you will eat fruit from your own vine and fig tree and drink water from your own cistern, until I come and take you to a land like your own — a land of grain and new wine, a land of bread and vineyards.
> "Do not let Hezekiah mislead you when he says, 'The LORD will deliver us.' Have the gods of any nations ever delivered their lands from the hand of the king of Assyria? Where are the gods of Hamath and Arpad? Where are the gods of Sepharvaim? Have they rescued Samaria from my hand? Who of all the gods of these countries have been able to save their lands from me? How then can the LORD deliver Jerusalem from my hand?"(Isaiah 36:13-20)

This supposed genius spoke foolish words against God and His people. He insulted and mocked the Lord through his words of intimidation. And it seems he was ignorant of the fact that the city of Nineveh had repented and turned to God years earlier.

The Bible tells us that after the commander spoke, no one said a word. King Hezekiah ordered that no one respond to his threats and demoralizing comments. "But the people remained silent and said nothing in reply, because the king had commanded, "Do not answer him"(Isaiah 36:21).

The Death of 185,000 Assyrians

When King Hezekiah heard what the Assyrian commander said, he was visibly upset. He tore his garment, put on a thick sackcloth, and went up to the temple. The king did very well to enter the temple and not leave the city. Had he mirrored the actions of his father Ahaz, Hezekiah would have kept on his royal robe and gone out of the palace to surrender to the enemy.

This was the one crisis Hezekiah knew he couldn't handle alone. He had no choice but to call in the prophet Isaiah for guidance. And from that time on, Hezekiah listened to all the prophet had to say and followed his advice.

Isaiah sent the following reply back to the king, "This is what the LORD says: Do not be afraid of what you have heard — those words with which the underlings of the king of Assyria have blasphemed me. Listen! When he hears a certain report, I will make him want to return to his own country, and there I will have him cut down with the sword"(Isaiah 37:6-7).

Although the Bible makes mention of the shameful message of apology Hezekiah sent to the king of Assyria, it also records his beautiful prayer to God.

> "LORD Almighty, the God of Israel, enthroned between the cherubim, you alone are God over all the kingdoms of the earth. You have made heaven and earth. Give ear, LORD, and hear; open your eyes, LORD, and see; listen to all the words Sennacherib has sent to ridicule the living God.
> It is true, LORD, that the Assyrian kings have laid waste all these peoples and their lands. They have thrown their gods into the fire and destroyed them, for they were not gods but only wood and stone, fashioned by human hands. Now, LORD our God, deliver us from his hand, so that all the kingdoms of the earth may know that you, LORD, are the only God"(Isaiah 37:16-20).

God heard the king's prayer and answered him through a message from the prophet Isaiah. In great detail, Isaiah shared that although the Assyrian king had already left for Judah, he would not be able to arrive in Jerusalem. He wouldn't even be able to shoot an arrow into or approach the city. He would have to return back home(see Isaiah 37:21-34).

In verse 35, we see that God would protect the city of Jerusalem "for the sake of David, my servant." Here's the history behind those words.

Bust of Herodotus
The Ancient Agora Museum

When David was king over the united nation of Israel, he noticed the ark of God was housed inside tent curtains. He thought the ark should have a better home than he, so he set about to build the Lord a temple. (The Scriptures I mentioned earlier about David's gifts and offerings were to this very temple.) Because David bestowed that honor to God, God promised that David's house and his throne would be secure forever — "Your royal house and your kingdom will last forever in my sight. Your throne will last forever"(2 Samuel 7:16).

That night God answered Hezekiah's prayer and all one hundred and eighty-five thousand soldiers of Assyria sent to destroy Jerusalem were killed. Imagine that! "Then the angel of the LORD went out and put to death a hundred and eighty-five thousand in the Assyrian camp. When the people got up the next morning — there were all the dead bodies!"(Isaiah 37:36).

Quoting Herodotus, historian Paul Johnson wrote that a plague of rats infested and ultimately killed the Assyrians.[19] Also quoting Herodotus, Flavius Josephus, the Jewish historian recorded, "Now when Sennacherib was returning from his Egyptian war to Jerusalem, he found his army under Rabshakeh his general, in danger by a plague, for God had sent a pestilential distemper upon his army; and on the very first night of the siege a hundred and eighty-five thousand, with their captains and generals were destroyed."[20] Josephus also wrote, "A multitude of mice gnawed to pieces in one night both the bows, and the rest of the armour of the Assyrians."[21]

At the unusual and tragic death of his soldiers, King Sennacherib had no other choice but to return to Assyria. He would end up being assassinated by two of his sons and succeeded in power by another(see 2 Kings 19:37 and Isaiah 37:38). It was the beginning of the end of the Assyrian Empire.

The Prophet Nahum

One hundred and fifty years earlier, the prophet Jonah preached to Nineveh, the capital of Assyria, and everyone including the king repented and were forgiven and saved by God. And one hundred and fifty years later,

A Stone Panel from the North-West Palace of Ashurnasirpal II _ The British Museum

Assyria fell. The same God who extended grace and mercy to a city through a prophet called Jonah declared a total destruction to that same city through a prophet named Nahum.

The book of Nahum begins, "A prophecy concerning Nineveh. The book of the vision of Nahum the Elkoshite" (Nahum 1:1). The prophet mentioned that the city would be destroyed with overflowing waters, and God would drive the Assyrians away in darkness. "But with an overwhelming flood he will make an end of Nineveh; he will pursue his foes into the realm of darkness" (Nahum 1:8). An "overwhelming flood" is the best way to describe Assyria's disappearance. (In the beginning of this chapter, I talked about how the Tigris River covered Nineveh and how dirt and sand were piled up on top of it, leaving no trace of the city, until Laynard's discovery.)

Let's look at more of Nahum's prophecy. The Lord said, "Although they have allies and are numerous, they will be destroyed and pass away. Although I have afflicted you, Judah, I will afflict you no more"(Nahum 1:12). In the next couple of verses, God specifically speaks to Assyria and says she will be no more.

> "King of Assyria, your shepherd slumber; your nobles lie down to rest. Your people are scattered on the mountains with no one

to gather them. Nothing can heal you; your wound is fatal. All who hear the news about you clap their hands at your fall, for who has not felt your endless cruelty?"(Nahum 3:18-19).

The Downfall of Assyrian Empire

Nineveh fell to Babylon in 612 BC, and the new Assyrian capital of Haran surrendered to the new empire in 610 BC. The Assyrian reign of power had been one of fear, domination, evil, and cruelty. The last king, Ashur-uballit II, died a violent death. He set fire to his palace and died in the flames. In 609 BC, Assyria finally gave up its territory of Upper Asia, which she maintained for five hundred and twenty years, to Babylon, the empire on the rise.

As prophesied by Nahum, the destruction of Assyria would be such delightful news to many nations of the ancient Near East they would figuratively applaud the demise. There was not one country in that area of the world that wasn't negatively affected by Assyria's tyrannical and vicious governing powers. Some of the empire's kings even proclaimed their own evil behavior.

In *The Luck of Nineveh,* Arnold C. Brackman wrote about the sayings of various Assyrian kings. King Ashurbanipal said, "I am merciless...first in war, king of the world...who has trampled down all who were not submissive to him, and who brought under his sway the totality of all people." King Shalmaneser called himself "the sun of all peoples, despot of all lands." King Tiglath-Pileser boasted, "42 countries and their kings...my hand conquered...and laid on them the heavy yoke of my rule." King Sennacherib called himself a "mighty hero clothed in terror." King Esarhaddon said that he was a "consuming, unquenchable fire...the unsparing weapon which

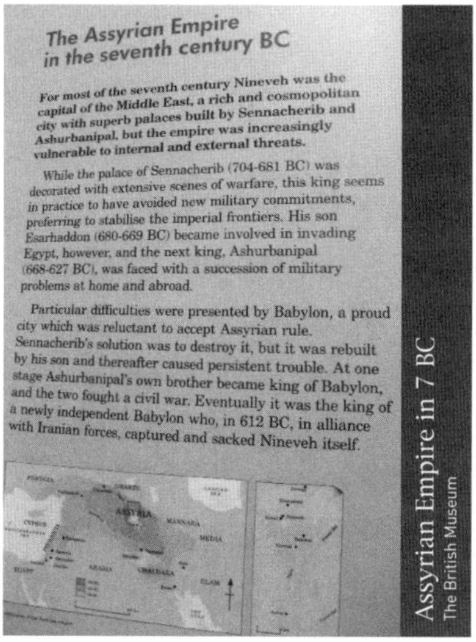

Assyrian Empire in 7 BC
The British Museum

utterly destroys the enemy's land." King Ashurbanipal described himself as a "terrible hurricane...who filled the plains...with blood." One Assyrian king, in avenging the revolt of a group of Egyptians said, "...not a man among them escaped...Their corpses I hung on stakes, I stripped off their skins and covered the city walls with them."

There was a big difference between how King David and the Assyrian kings ruled. Unlike King David, those kings were arrogant, cruel, and did not fear God. King Shalmaneser said that he was "the sun of all people and king of all countries;" David said in Psalm 23 that the Lord is his shepherd. King Ashurbanipal said, "I trampled under foot all those who did not surrender and put all people of the world in my crutches." David prayed, "You have established your people Israel as your very own forever, and you, LORD, have become their God" (2 Samuel 7:24).

The difference between these two kinds of leadership is polar-opposite. King David, even when he ascended the throne, was not consumed with power. He understood he was a servant of the kingdom of God and, therefore, humbly served God's people, the people of Israel.

God's Management of the Universe

A keyword I connect with the management of the Assyrian empire is "boundary." Assyria invaded the boundaries of other countries, destroyed each nation's uniqueness and individuality, and made the citizens of different nations live in mixed communities. The Assyrians perpetuated this type of dominance to expand their empire and weaken individual nations and, thereby, proactively eliminated any possible uprising or revolt against the empire.

The boundaries, or borders, of a nation are not something that can be reorganized. It is God who created every nation and established their boundaries from the beginning of time. The heavy feet of an army or an iron hand of tyranny should not be what tramples over borders; the Gospel of Good News is what should joyfully spread over all nations. This is something we should never forget.

It was God who told Jonah to declare the Word of salvation to the people of Nineveh and as a result saved one hundred and twenty thousand of its citizens and livestock from destruction. It was God who protected the boundary of Jerusalem when Assyria intended to attack Judah. It was God who said that the boundary of land Assyria could take stretched no further than the city of Samaria.

The Apostle Paul in the New Testament also declared how God determines boundaries. "From one man he made all the nations, that they should inhabit the whole earth; and he marked out their appointed times in history and the boundaries of their lands"(Acts 17:26). The book of Job tells us how God decides even the boundary of seas.

> "Who shut up the sea behind doors when it burst forth from the womb, when I made the clouds its garment and wrapped it in thick darkness, when I fixed limits for it and set its doors and bars in place, when I said, 'This far you may come and no farther; here is where your proud waves halt'?"(Job 38:8-11).

No matter how powerful a nation or empire is, it is God and God alone who manages the world. And it is God who determines the boundaries of all things — nations, seas, and even time. In the words of Isaiah, "The LORD Almighty has sworn, "Surely, as I have planned, so it will be, and as I have purposed, so it will happen. I will crush the Assyrian in my land; on my mountains I will trample him down. His yoke will be taken from my people, and his burden removed from their shoulders." This is the plan determined for the whole world; this is the hand stretched out over all nations. For the LORD Almighty has purposed, and who can thwart him? His hand is stretched out, and who can turn it back?"(Isaiah 14:24-27).

CHAPTER 2
BIBLE with BABYLONIAN EMPIRE

The books of the Bible related to Babylon

Jeremiah, Lamentations, Daniel, Ezekiel, Habakkuk, Zephaniah, II Kings, II Chronicles etc.

King Hezekiah and the Messengers from Babylon

The Babylonian Empire is unique in that there are more mentions of her in the Bible than the other empires. Yet there is less evidence and fewer records of her outside of Biblical references. However, I believe the Biblical account of this empire is sufficient to learn about her.

Babylon was a special and prosperous nation that began around 2000 BC. It is the dynasty that established Hammurabi's Code, instituted by the sixth king of the same name who ruled from 1792 to 1750 BC.

After King Sennacherib and the Assyrian army were defeated, King Hezekiah fell deathly ill. The prophet Isaiah, fearing he would not live, suggested he write his will(see Isaiah 38:1). The king, however, did not give up hope and prayed to God. "Remember, Lord, how I have walked before you faithfully and with wholehearted devotion and have done what is good in your eyes. And Hezekiah wept bitterly"(Isaiah 38:3). (Historian Flavius Josephus speculated that Hezekiah cried not because he was sick but because he regretted that he had no heir.[22)])

God heard his prayer. "Then the word of the LORD came to Isaiah:

Merodach-Baladan
Altes Museum

'Go and tell Hezekiah, This is what the LORD, the God of your father David, says: I have heard your prayer and seen your tears; I will add fifteen years to your life'"(Isaiah 3:4-5). In those fifteen years, the king produced an heir(see 2 Kings 21:1).

The news that King Hezekiah had been healed traveled throughout the ancient Near East. When the Babylonian king, Marduk-Baladan, received the report, he dispatched envoys to Judah to visit him(see Isaiah 39:1). King Hezekiah was happy to be receiving the attention because at the time, Babylon was an empire on the rise and Assyria's biggest threat. Though Babylon had been under the rule of Assyria, she was strengthening her power in order to one day dominate the ancient Near East.

When the one hundred and eighty-five thousand Assyrian troops were destroyed, it was obvious to other countries that the Babylonian Empire was the one rapidly gaining power and strength. That's why King Hezekiah was thrilled to welcome the Babylonian envoys. "Hezekiah received the envoys gladly and showed them what was in his storehouses — the silver, the gold, the spices, the fine olive oil — his entire armory and everything found among his treasures. There was nothing in his palace or in all his kingdom that Hezekiah did not show them"(Isaiah 39:2).

King Hezekiah's boasting was a mistake. He was claiming credit for the defeat of the Assyrians, which had been a miracle performed by God. Instead of testifying about God's power in the stunning victory, he tried to impress the Babylonians with his power and wealth. The Babylonians would later use all they were shown to their advantage when they would invade Judah.

The Prophet Isaiah

When he heard the news that the Babylonian envoys had visited, Isaiah became suspicious and went to see Hezekiah. The prophet asked the king for details, which he willingly shared.

> Then Isaiah the prophet went to King Hezekiah and asked, "What did those men say, and where did they come from?"
> "From a distant land," Hezekiah replied. "They came to me from Babylon."
> The prophet asked, "What did they see in your palace?"
> "They saw everything in my palace," Hezekiah said. "There is nothing among my treasures that I did not show them."
> Then Isaiah said to Hezekiah, "Hear the word of the LORD Almighty: The time will surely come when everything in your palace, and all that your predecessors have stored up until this day, will be carried off to Babylon. Nothing will be left, says the LORD. And some of your descendants, your own flesh and blood who will be born to you, will be taken away, and they will become eunuchs in the palace of the king of Babylon."
> "The word of the LORD you have spoken is good," Hezekiah replied. For he thought, "There will be peace and security in my lifetime."(Isaiah 39:3-8)

God was saying through Isaiah that the Babylonian Empire would eventually destroy Judah. This was different than Isaiah's earlier prophecies, which spoke of how his country would be delivered from the Assyrian Empire. Now he had to speak of the destruction of his country at the hands of the Babylonians. You can imagine how conflicted the prophet must have felt having to utter a prophecy that was against his own people.

The last words of King Hezekiah recorded in the Bible — "The word of the LORD you have spoken is good..." — do not depict him in a flattering light. His relief that destruction would not come during his reign was a sign of pride and arrogance.

Babylon and the Three Captivities of Israel

After King Hezekiah died in 686 BC, his twelve-year-old son Manasseh became king of Judah and ruled for fifty-five years. During his reign, he perpetrated all kinds of evil. King Manasseh rebuilt altars for idols, served Baal and Asherah, and appointed mediums and wizards(see 2 Kings 21:6). God was angry at the kingdom of Judah because of the evildoings of the king.

"Neither before nor after Josiah was there a king like him who

King Josiah _by Julius Schnorr von Carolsfeld

> turned to the LORD as he did — with all his heart and with all his soul and with all his strength, in accordance with all the Law of Moses. Nevertheless, the LORD did not turn away from the heat of his fierce anger, which burned against Judah because of all that Manasseh had done to arouse his anger"(2 Kings 23:25-26).

When King Manasseh's evil was too much to take, God took him away to Babylon. When he repented, God returned him to Judah to continue his reign.

> "So the LORD brought against them the army commanders of the king of Assyria, who took Manasseh prisoner, put a hook in his nose, bound him with bronze shackles and took him to Babylon. In his distress he sought the favor of the LORD his God and humbled himself greatly before the God of his ancestors. And when he prayed to him, the LORD was moved by his entreaty and listened to his plea; so he brought him back to Jerusalem and to his kingdom. Then Manasseh knew that the LORD is God" (2 Chronicles 33:11-13).

Bricks used in Nebuchadnezzar's Age
The British Museum

After Manasseh, Amon became king. After Amon, Josiah became king of Judah.

As I mentioned in the first chapter, King Josiah was a great king who pleased God and followed after the ways of King David. He was killed during the battle against Pharaoh Necho of Egypt in Megiddo in an attempt to gain the favor of Babylonian King Nabopolassar. After

Josiah's death, the people of Judah made Jehoahaz, his son, the new king. However, Egypt dethroned Jehoahaz and made Jehoahaz's brother, Jehoiakim, king. Jehoahaz was taken to Egypt where he was killed.

During his reign, Jehoiakim switched alliances from Egypt to Babylon and back to Egypt, and consequently Babylon moved to attack both Judah and Egypt (see the below passage as well as verse 7).

> "During Jehoiakim's reign, Nebuchadnezzar king of Babylon invaded the land, and Jehoiakim became his vassal for three years. But then he turned against Nebuchadnezzar and rebelled. The LORD sent Babylonian, Aramean, Moabite and Ammonite raiders against him to destroy Judah, in accordance with the word of the LORD proclaimed by his servants the prophets. Surely these things happened to Judah according to the LORD's command, in order to remove them from his presence because of the sins of Manasseh and all he had done, including the shedding of innocent blood. For he had filled Jerusalem with innocent blood, and the LORD was not willing to forgive"(2 Kings 24:1-4).

During this time, Babylon took captive the people of Judah on three

The Babylonian Chronicles recorded in an Ancient Babylonian Tablet
The British Museum

separate occasions — 605 BC, 598 BC, and 586 BC. In 605 BC Babylon took away a number of Hebrew scholars and artisans, including the young Daniel and three of his friends. This was known as the first Babylonian captivity. King Nebuchadnezzar wanted Hebrew young men to learn Babylonian culture and laws so they could lead and teach others in the ways of Babylon.

King Nebuchadnezzar also was looking for specific people to work for him in his palace. "Then the king ordered Ashpenaz, chief of his court officials, to bring into the king's service some of the Israelites from the royal family and the nobility — young men without any physical defect, handsome, showing aptitude for every kind of learning, well informed, quick to understand, and qualified to serve in the king's palace. He was to teach them the language and literature of the Babylonians"(Daniel 1:3-4).

This is a great example of Babylonian imperialism. I suspect the Babylonians invested more time and effort into the leadership of their empire than in construction or any other projects. When the Assyrians were in power, their path to imperialism was to intermingle different races into one community. But Babylon, the new world power, opted to use education to maintain control of all the territories under her rule. A similar form of this imperialistic rule was later adopted by the Roman Empire and the British Empire.

A few years before the second Babylonian captivity, the Babylonians captured King Jehoiakim and took him to Babylon(see 2 Chronicles 36:5-6) where he died shortly thereafter. His eighteen-year-old son Jehoiachin ascended to the throne but lasted only three months before the Babylonians invaded again.

In 598 BC, the second Babylonian captivity took place. Ten thousand people from Jerusalem, including the prophet Ezekiel and King Jehoiachin, were taken away to Babylon to work as engineers to make the city the greatest in the world. Babylon then appointed Zedekiah, Jehoiachin's uncle, as the last king of Judah.

The Hebrews constantly complained to God and wished they could return to Jerusalem. But the prophet Ezekiel told them that Jerusalem would be destroyed and they would be held captive for seventy years. He advised them to follow the laws of God and build good lives in Babylon until the time when their descendents could go back to Judah.

By this time, the only Hebrews who remained in Judah were those less skilled and less educated, and most of them were taken during the third Babylonian captivity in 586 BC. Nebuzaradan, the captain of the Babylonian guard, left only a small number in Jerusalem to take care of the vineyards and farms.

The Babylonians also destroyed the temple in the Judean city and stole the treasures inside God's house. The enemy soldiers "broke up the bronze pillars, the movable stands and the bronze Sea that were at the temple of the LORD and they carried the bronze to Babylon. They also took away the pots, shovels, wick trimmers, dishes and all the bronze articles used in the temple service. The commander of the imperial guard took away the censers and sprinkling bowls — all that were made of pure gold or silver"(2 Kings 25:13-14).

I like to explore in detail some of the important Biblical characters, Daniel, Ezekiel, and Jeremiah, who made history during these captivities.

Daniel and Ezekiel the captives

When Daniel and his three friends, Hananiah, Mishael, and Azariah, were taken captive during the first captivity, their names were changed to Beltshazzar, Shadrach, Meshach, and Abednego. Along with their peers, these men went through an intensive three-year education course. It was as demanding as getting a doctorate is today. Their diets, too, were dictated by the king, who decided which particular foods they could consume.

Remaining steadfast in his personal convictions, Daniel requested that he be allowed to eat according to the laws prescribed by God. He posed a challenge to the government officials. "Please test your servants for ten days: Give us nothing but vegetables to eat and water to drink. Then compare our appearance with that of the young men who eat the royal food, and treat your servants in accordance with what you see"(Daniel 1:12-13).

Daniel and his three friends excelled in their studies and learned well the laws and ways of Babylon. "To these four young men God gave knowledge and understanding of all kinds of literature and learning. And Daniel could understand visions and dreams of all kinds"(Daniel 1:17). The latter part of this passage had great significance for Daniel and the empire of Babylon.

Like Pharaoh of Egypt, the Babylonian King Nebuchadnezzar, who held the throne at the time, had a disturbing dream. "In the second year of his reign, Nebuchadnezzar had dreams; his mind was troubled and he could not sleep"(Daniel 2:1). Unlike Pharaoh, however, Nebuchadnezzar didn't share his dream with anyone. Instead, he demanded that the sorcerers and magicians of his kingdom tell him the dream and also interpret it. He then threatened them. "This is what I have firmly decided: If you do not tell me what my dream was and interpret it, I will have you cut into pieces and your houses turned into piles of rubble"(Daniel 2:5).

Much to the king's dismay, his astrologers were unable to guess and interpret his dream.

> The astrologers answered the king, "There is no one on earth who can do what the king asks! No king, however great and mighty, has ever asked such a thing of any magician or enchanter or astrologer. What the king asks is too difficult. No one can reveal it to the king except the gods, and they do not live among humans." This made the king so angry and furious that he ordered the execution of all the wise men of Babylon. So the decree was issued to put the wise men to death, and men were sent to look for Daniel and his friends to put them to death"(Daniel 2:10-13).

The Feast _by Paul Cezanne

Daniel approached the king and asked him for more time so he could interpret the dream for him. Having studied the law and the records of Moses, Daniel remembered the story of Joseph, who had been in a similar situation. Joseph had said that dream interpretation came from God(see Genesis 40:8). So Daniel prayed. God heard Daniel and that night appeared to him in a vision, revealing the mystery of the king's dream. Because his prayer had been answered, Daniel gave God the praise.

"Praise be to the name of God for ever and ever; wisdom and power are his. He changes times and seasons; he deposes kings and raises up others. He gives wisdom to the wise and knowledge to the discerning. He reveals deep and hidden things; he knows what lies in darkness, and light dwells with him. I thank and praise you, God of my ancestors: You have given me wisdom and power, you have made known to me what we asked of you, you have made known to us the dream of the king"(Daniel 2:20-23).

Daniel then went to the king and told him about the dream. "Your Majesty looked, and there before you stood a large statue — an enormous, dazzling statue, awesome in appearance. The head of the statue was made of pure gold, its chest and arms of silver, its belly and thighs of bronze, its legs of iron, its feet partly of iron and partly of baked clay. While you were watching, a rock was cut out, but not by human hands. It struck the statue on its feet of iron and clay and smashed them. Then the iron, the clay, the bronze, the silver and the gold were all broken to pieces and became like chaff on a threshing floor in the summer. The wind swept them away without leaving a trace. But the rock that struck the statue became a huge mountain and filled the whole earth"(Daniel 2:31-35). (I wonder whether the statue in the dream was a mix of Ironman and the Tin Man.)

Next Daniel revealed the meaning of the dream to the Babylonian king(see Daniel 2:36-45). He related the parts of the statue to various future empires, which we now know represented the kingdoms of Persia, Greece, and Rome. He also spoke about the rise and downfall of each one, beginning with Babylon.

King Nebuchadnezzar was humbled at Daniel's revelation and especially at his ability to tell the king his own dream without any hints. The king bowed down before Daniel and showered him with gifts and incense. It was a strange spectacle to see this terrible tyrant acknowledging the God Daniel served and even confessing that He is the one true God. "Surely your God is the God of gods and the Lord of kings and a revealer of mysteries, for you were able to reveal this mystery"(Daniel 2:47).

This was a pivotal event for Daniel and his three friends. The king appointed Daniel ruler over all the districts of Babylon and made him the highest person among all the wise men in the city. Daniel was made to stay in the king's palace. Also, at Daniel's request, the king arranged for his three friends to serve as administrators.

Although Daniel had been taken captive and educated in the ways of Babylon, he lived according to the laws of God, even maintaining a diet in line with his religious beliefs. Daniel is a wonderful example of a person who resolves to live according to the Word of God.

Daniel's godly lifestyle reflected his knowledge that all empires are in God's hands and only the eternal kingdom of God is worth serving. King Nebuchadnezzar's dream confirmed to Daniel that God is in control of the world, not powerful people, countries, or governments. After all, Daniel knew that the empire of Babylon would be destroyed in seventy years. "In the first year of his reign, I, Daniel, understood from the Scriptures, according to the word of the LORD given to Jeremiah the prophet, that the desolation of Jerusalem would last seventy years"(Daniel 9:2).

God gave unique insight to Daniel about the management of empires, as he lived under the rule of three different empires. At a young age, Daniel saw the destruction of the Assyrian Empire at the hands of Babylon and the subsequent expansion of the Babylonian Empire. He also witnessed Babylon's destruction. Daniel was later appointed to a high position of power within the Persian Empire that followed. We must not forget that Daniel was first and foremost a prophet, appointed by God to preach His Word, even as he carried out his responsibilities in kings' palaces at the height of the Babylonian Empire and the subsequent Persian Empire.

I'd like to briefly touch on Daniel's role in the Persian Empire. Daniel 6 tells us how he came to power under the rule of King Darius. "It pleased Darius to appoint 120 satraps to rule throughout the kingdom, with three administrators over them, one of whom was Daniel. The satraps were made accountable to them so that the king might not suffer loss. Now Daniel so distinguished himself among the administrators and the satraps by his exceptional qualities that the king planned to set him over the whole kingdom"(Daniel 6:1-3).

Daniel's Answer to the King
by Briton Rivière

When Daniel was given the opportunity to be the senior governor, his two colleagues were jealous and sought to find fault with him. However, they could not find any reason to disqualify him from this position so they moved to trap him(see Daniel 6:4-8). They made a law that the people of Persia could not bow down or pray to anyone or anything other than King Darius. Those who disobeyed would be thrown into the lion's den. They knew Daniel would not submit to anyone except God, so they were convinced this trick would work and get him in trouble with the king. True to his character, and even knowing full well that breaking this law would result in punishment, Daniel continued to pray to God three times a day(see Daniel 6:10).

King Darius soon realized the malicious intentions of the officials who put this wicked decree into law and was very upset at learning of Daniel's punishment. The king stayed up all night fasting and praying for his safe return. Daniel was such a loyal subject, and King Darius had a deep respect for him. Daniel had been faithful to both the king and to God; his loyalty served him well.

Daniel, of course, was delivered from the lion's den. The Bible tells us of how King Darius honored God as a result of the miraculous deliverance. "I issue a decree that in every part of my kingdom people must fear and reverence the God of Daniel. For he is the living God and he endures forever; his kingdom will not be destroyed, his dominion will never end. He rescues and he saves; he performs signs and wonders in the heavens and on the earth. He has rescued Daniel from the power of the lions"(Daniel 6:26-27).

The Second Captivity and the Prophet Ezekiel

A twenty-five-year old priest named Ezekiel was part of the group of ten thousand Hebrews taken to Babylon in the second captivity in 598 BC.

The book of Ezekiel begins with the fifth year of his Babylonian captivity. "In my thirtieth year, in the fourth month on the fifth day, while I was among the exiles by the Kebar River, the heavens were opened and I saw visions of God. On the fifth of the month — it was the fifth year of the exile of King Jehoiachin — the word of the LORD came to Ezekiel the priest, the son of Buzi, by the Kebar River in the land of the Babylonians. There the hand of the LORD was on him"(Ezekiel 1:1-3).

The Word of the Lord was that the people of the second captivity would live a few decades in Babylon and should comfort the people of the third captivity (see Ezekiel 37). Ezekiel encouraged his fellow captives to settle peacefully in Babylon and to lead happy, godly lives in preparation for the day when they would return to Jerusalem. But it wasn't easy for Ezekiel to preach this message of hope to those who believed they had been captured because God was not powerful enough to secure their freedom. They also believed that their ancestors had committed evil and they were being unjustly punished for those past sins. But as explained by the Word given through the prophet Jeremiah (I'll talk about him later), God sent His people to Babylon not to destroy them but to give them hope for the future.

> "For I know the plans I have for you," declares the LORD, "plans to prosper you and not to harm you, plans to give you hope and a future. Then you will call on me and come and pray to me, and I will listen to you. You will seek me and find me when you seek me with all your heart. I will be found by you," declares the LORD, "and will bring you back from captivity. I will gather you from all the nations and places where I have banished you," declares the LORD, "and will bring you back to the place from which I carried you into exile"(Jeremiah 29:11-14).

Twelve years after their captivity, Ezekiel prophesied about the fall of

Jerusalem. "In the twelfth year of our exile, in the tenth month on the fifth day, a man who had escaped from Jerusalem came to me and said, "The city has fallen!" Now the evening before the man arrived, the hand of the Lord was on me, and he opened my mouth before the man came to me in the morning. So my mouth was opened and I was no longer silent"(Ezekiel 33:21-22).

After Jerusalem was completely destroyed, the people of Judah finally listened to Ezekiel.

Jeremiah, the True Prophet of God, and the False Prophet Hananiah

The prophet Jeremiah, who lived and served God at the same time as Ezekiel, preached out of Jerusalem. He was called the "weeping prophet" because he wept a great deal for the present and future conditions of the people of God. Jeremiah's message, similar to Ezekiel's, was that the sooner they surrendered to Babylon, the easier and better their lives would be.

And just like Ezekiel, the people of Judah did not accept Jeremiah's message. They also accused Jeremiah of being pro-Babylon. They hated him for what they believed was a betrayal of Judah, they threatened him with violence, and they even put him in prison. The following passages of Scripture from the book of Jeremiah reveal the heartbreaking life of this prophet.

> "Should good be repaid with evil? Yet they have dug a pit for me. Remember that I stood before you and spoke in their behalf to turn your wrath away from them"(Jeremiah 18:20).

> "He had Jeremiah the prophet beaten and put in the stocks at the Upper Gate of Benjamin at the LORD's temple"(Jeremiah 20:2).

> "They were angry with Jeremiah and had him beaten and imprisoned in the house of Jonathan the secretary, which they had made into a prison. Jeremiah was put into a vaulted cell in a dungeon, where he remained a long time"(Jeremiah 37:15-16).

> "So they took Jeremiah and put him into the cistern of Malkijah, the king's son, which was in the courtyard of the guard. They lowered Jeremiah by ropes into the cistern; it had no water in it, only mud, and Jeremiah sank down into the mud"(Jeremiah 38:6).

Because the conditions of his life were so horrible, Jeremiah almost abandoned his call, but ultimately he just could not keep God's message locked inside his heart. He wrote, "You deceived me, Lord, and I was deceived; you overpowered me and prevailed. I am ridiculed all day long; everyone mocks me. Whenever I speak, I cry out proclaiming violence and destruction. So the word of the Lord has brought me insult and reproach all day long. But if I say, "I will not mention his word or speak anymore in his name," his word is in my heart like a fire, a fire shut up in my bones. I am weary of holding it in; indeed, I cannot"(Jeremiah 20:7-9).

What made Jeremiah's job as a prophet even more painful were the false testimonies of phony prophets. He warned the people of these phonies. "Then the Lord said to me, "The prophets are prophesying lies in my name. I have not sent them or appointed them or spoken to them. They are prophesying to you false visions, divinations, idolatries and the delusions of their own minds. Therefore this is what the Lord says about the prophets who are prophesying in my name: I did not send them, yet they are saying, 'No sword or famine will touch this land.' Those same

prophets will perish by sword and famine. And the people they are prophesying to will be thrown out into the streets of Jerusalem because of the famine and sword. There will be no one to bury them, their wives, their sons and their daughters. I will pour out on them the calamity they deserve"(Jeremiah 14:14-16).

During the reign of King Zedekiah, the last king of Judah, a false prophet by the name of Hananiah gathered together a huge crowd of priests and people in the temple. This is what he told them. "In the fifth month of that same year, the fourth year, early in the reign of Zedekiah king of Judah, the prophet Hananiah son of Azzur, who was from Gibeon, said to me in the house of the LORD in the presence of the priests and all the people: "This is what the LORD Almighty, the God of Israel, says: 'I will break the yoke of the king of Babylon. Within two years I will bring back to this place all the articles of the LORD's house that Nebuchadnezzar king of Babylon removed from here and took to Babylon. I will also bring back to this place Jehoiachin son of Jehoiakim king of Judah and all the other exiles from Judah who went to Babylon,' declares the LORD, 'for I will break the yoke of the king of Babylon'"(Jeremiah 28:1-4).

This message was nothing but lies. In that time, the Hebrews from both the first and second captivities were in Babylon. Hananiah falsely predicted that God would destroy Babylon in two years and all the captives and temple furnishings would be returned to their rightful place. They were encouraged at this message, but God's Word was clear. The Hebrews would be captive to the Babylonian Empire for seventy years, not two. This was the true message of the Lord:

> "Build houses and settle down; plant gardens and eat what they produce. Marry and have sons and daughters; find wives for your sons and give your daughters in marriage, so that they too may have sons and daughters. Increase in number there; do not decrease. Also, seek the peace and prosperity of the city to which I have carried you into exile. Pray to the LORD for it, because if it prospers, you too will prosper." Yes, this is what the LORD Almighty, the God of Israel, says: "Do not let the prophets and diviners among you deceive you. Do not listen to the dreams you encourage them to have. They are prophesying lies to you in my name. I have not sent them," declares the LORD. This is what the LORD says: "When seventy years are completed for Babylon, I will come to you and fulfill my good promise to bring you back to this place"(Jeremiah 29:5-10).

God told Jeremiah that Hananiah would die that year. "Therefore this is what the LORD says: 'I am about to remove you from the face of the earth. This very year you are going to die, because you have preached rebellion against the LORD'"(Jeremiah 28:16-17). True to the Word of the Lord, this false prophet died in the seventh month of that year.

The Meaning Behind Seventy Years of Captivity

Why did God, a mathematical genius, deliberately choose seventy years as the length of time for the captivity? When the Israelites entered the Promised Land after leaving Egypt, the book of Leviticus tells us that they were to observe the Sabbath, sabbatical years, and Jubilees.

Concerning the Sabbath, God said, "There are six days when you may work, but the seventh day is a day of Sabbath rest, a day of sacred assembly. You are not to do any work; wherever you live, it is a Sabbath to the LORD" (Leviticus 23:3).

Concerning the sabbatical year, God said, "Speak to the Israelites and say to them: 'When you enter the land I am going to give you, the land itself must observe a sabbath to the LORD. For six years sow your fields, and for six years prune your vineyards and gather their crops. But in the seventh year the land is to have a year of sabbath rest, a sabbath to the LORD. Do not sow your fields or prune your vineyards. Do not reap what grows of itself or harvest the grapes of your untended vines. The land is to have a year of rest"(Leviticus 25:2-5).

Concerning the Jubilee, God said, "Count off seven sabbath years — seven times seven years — so that the seven sabbath years amount to a period of forty-nine years. Then have the trumpet sounded everywhere on the tenth day of the seventh month; on the Day of Atonement sound the trumpet throughout your land. Consecrate the fiftieth year and proclaim liberty throughout the land to all its inhabitants. It shall be a jubilee for you; each of you is to return to your family property and to your own clan. The fiftieth year shall be a jubilee for you; do not sow and do not reap what grows of itself or harvest the untended vines. For it is a jubilee and is to be holy for you; eat only what is taken directly from the fields"(Leviticus 25:8-12).

The women of Israel taken captive to Babylon
by Charles Zacharie Landelle

In the twenty-sixth chapter of

Leviticus, God warned that if Israel would not observe these important religious occasions, the land would get the rest it required and the people would be subject to their enemies. "But if you will not listen to me and carry out all these commands...Then the land will enjoy its sabbath years all the time that it lies desolate and you are in the country of your enemies; then the land will rest and enjoy its sabbaths. All the time that it lies desolate, the land will have the rest it did not have during the sabbaths you lived in it"(Leviticus 26:14, 34-35).

When the Israelites lived in Canaan for two hundred and thirty years, they did not observe the Sabbath, sabbatical year, or jubilee until King Zedekiah was on the throne. Therefore, God counted all those days and said that he would give rest to the land for seventy years. "He carried into exile to Babylon the remnant, who escaped from the sword, and they became servants to him and his successors until the kingdom of Persia came to power. The land enjoyed its sabbath rests; all the time of its desolation it rested, until the seventy years were completed in fulfillment of the word of the LORD spoken by Jeremiah"(2 Chronicles 36:20-21).

Secret Meeting between King and Prophet

While Jeremiah was imprisoned by the high officials of Judah in the house of Jonathan the secretary King Zedekiah sent for him, and they had a private discussion in the palace. The king asked Jeremiah if he had a message from God, to which Jeremiah relayed that God would deliver Zedekiah into the hands of the Babylonian king(see Jeremiah 37:17). The prophet then begged not to be sent back to the house of Jonathan. The king obliged his request, and Jeremiah remained imprisoned in the palace.

> "What crime have I committed against you or your attendants or this people, that you have put me in prison? Where are your prophets who prophesied to you, 'The king of Babylon will not attack you or this land'? But now, my lord the king, please listen. Let me bring my petition before you: Do not send me back to the house of Jonathan the secretary, or I will die there." King Zedekiah then gave orders for Jeremiah to be placed in the courtyard of the guard and given a loaf of bread from the street of the bakers each day until all the bread in the city was gone. So Jeremiah remained in the courtyard of the guard(Jeremiah 37:18-21).

Jeremiah continued to trumpet God's message of how Jerusalem was going to be handed over to the Babylonian army. Those who opposed the prophet got even angrier and threw him into a cistern in the courtyard to die. Fortunately, Ebed-Melech, a Cushite palace official, heard about what happened to Jeremiah and told the king, "My lord the king, these men have acted wickedly in all they have done to Jeremiah the prophet. They have thrown him into a cistern, where he will starve to death when there is no longer any bread in the city"(Jeremiah 38:9).

When the king heard the news, he told Ebed-Melech, "Take thirty men from here with you and lift Jeremiah the prophet out of the cistern before he dies"(Jeremiah 38:10). Ebed-Melech obeyed the king's command. He "took the men with him and went to a room under the treasury in the palace. He took some old rags and worn-out clothes from there and let them down with ropes to Jeremiah in the cistern. Ebed-Melek the Cushite said to Jeremiah, "Put these old rags and worn-out clothes under your arms to pad the ropes." Jeremiah did so, and they pulled him up with the ropes and lifted him out of the cistern. And Jeremiah remained in the courtyard of the guard"(Jeremiah 38:11-13).

King Zedekiah wanted to confirm the will of God once more and sent for Jeremiah. The prophet was frightened the king would kill him, but Zedekiah promised to spare his life(see Jeremiah 38:16). Jeremiah spoke the words of the Lord, "This is what the LORD God Almighty, the God of Israel, says: 'If you surrender to the officers of the king of Babylon, your life will be spared and this city will not be burned down; you and your family will live. But if you will not surrender to the officers of the king of Babylon, this city will be given into the hands of the Babylonians and they will burn it down; you yourself will not escape from them'"(Jeremiah 38:17-18).

Though King Zedekiah wanted to surrender to Babylon, he was scared of how the people of Judah would react and how badly they would mistreat him. He threatened Jeremiah to keep the meeting a secret(see Jeremiah 38:24). Because the king cared more about his reputation with the people of his kingdom than about his reputation with God, he would ignore Jeremiah's warning and ultimately experience a horrible end to his reign.

King Zedekiah and His Sons' Tragic Fate

As Jeremiah prophesied, Babylon surrounded Jerusalem in 588 BC. They could not, however, immediately occupy the city, which shows what a mighty stronghold she was. King Nebuchadnezzar demanded King Zedekiah's surrender, saying that he would treat him with respect if he did. Zedekiah refused to listen to the conciliation of the Babylonian king or Jeremiah's past advice and remained in the city for eighteen months. And for eighteen months, the Babylonian army camped outside Jerusalem and waited for her voluntary surrender.

The time came when the Babylonian army attacked the city. "In the ninth year of Zedekiah king of Judah, in the tenth month, Nebuchadnezzar king of Babylon marched against Jerusalem with his whole army and laid

Slaughter of the Sons of Zedekiah before their Father
by Gustave Dore

siege to it. And on the ninth day of the fourth month of Zedekiah's eleventh year, the city wall was broken through"(Jeremiah 39:1-2).

When King Zedekiah saw the approaching army, he ran off. According to the record of Flavius Josephus, the king fled to the desert through a trench together with his family, friends, and close subjects. But someone relayed the information to the Babylonians, and the invading army chased the king down and eventually captured him near Jericho.[23)]

King Zedekiah was brought to the king of Babylon for questioning(see Jeremiah 39:4-5). There the unthinkable happened. His two young sons were beheaded right in front of their father(see Jeremiah 39:6-7). (We know the two sons who were murdered were young because Zedekiah was only thirty-two years old at the time.)

Zedekiah's royal subjects were also killed, and the king's eyes were gouged out, a common form of torture to kings who refused to surrender before they were ultimately invaded.[24)] The king took great pride in his reputation only to pay for it with the lives of his sons and others.

King Jehoiachin, who was taken to Babylon during the second captivity, was eventually released and exalted to a high position. "In the thirty-seventh year of the exile of Jehoiachin king of Judah, in the year Awel-Marduk became king of Babylon, on the twenty-fifth day of the twelfth month, he released Jehoiachin king of Judah and freed him from prison. He spoke kindly to him and gave him a seat of honor higher than those of the other kings who were with him in Babylon. So Jehoiachin put aside his prison clothes and for the rest of his life ate regularly at the king's table. Day by day the king of Babylon gave Jehoiachin a regular allowance as long as he lived, till the day of his death"(Jeremiah 52:31-34).

A portrait of Josephus
(from a book of William Whiston)

I wonder if King Zedekiah had heeded Jeremiah's advice, if he would have been treated like King Jehoiachin. Perhaps he would have been spared such a brutal end and granted favor.

The Destruction of the Jerusalem Temple and the Sketch of the New Temple

During the attack on Jerusalem, the temple was destroyed and the third group of captives was taken to Babylon. "The Babylonians set fire to the royal palace and the houses of the people and broke down the walls of Jerusalem. Nebuzaradan commander of the imperial guard carried into exile to Babylon the people who remained in the city, along with those who had gone over to him, and the rest of the people. But Nebuzaradan the commander of the guard left behind in the land of Judah some of the poor people, who owned nothing; and at that time he gave them vineyards and fields"(Jeremiah 39:8-10).

The book of Jeremiah records another account of this siege in Chapter 52. "On the tenth day of the fifth month, in the nineteenth year of Nebuchadnezzar king of Babylon, Nebuzaradan commander of the imperial guard, who served the king of Babylon, came to Jerusalem. He set fire to the temple of the LORD, the royal palace and all the houses of Jerusalem. Every important building he burned down. The whole Babylonian army, under the commander of the imperial guard, broke down all the walls around Jerusalem"(Jeremiah 52:12-14).

Pillage is commonly associated with war in ancient times and even today. Known as the spoils of war, these atrocious acts were done to buttress soldiers' morale. Pillage was very violent and bloody, and most victims were women and children. Sometimes the barbarities continued for days.

The city of Jerusalem experienced the abominableness of pillage. All of Jerusalem was on fire. It was a broken city. Dead bodies filled the streets along with the rubble of destroyed buildings. Jeremiah was devastated at the sight of such destruction. He even saw a baby sucking at the breast of its mother; the mother was dead and the baby was sucking the blood out of her. It was such a horrible sight; the prophet could not stop crying. "My eyes fail from weeping, I am in torment within; my heart is poured out on the ground because my people are destroyed, because children and infants faint in the streets of the city"(Lamentations 2:11).

The weeping prophet mourned all night for the destroyed city of Jerusalem. When morning came, however, his mood had changed. He praised God with all his might. Jeremiah felt thankful because he discovered a shining ray of hope that all had not been destroyed; some of the people had survived.

> "I remember my affliction and my wandering, the bitterness and the gall. I well remember them, and my soul is downcast within me. Yet this I call to mind and therefore I have hope: Because of the LORD's great love we are not consumed, for his compassions never fail. They are new every morning; great is your faithfulness"
> (Lamentations 3:19-23).

At the same time that Jeremiah was witnessing the desolation of Jerusalem, despair was unfolding in Babylon as predicted in Ezekiel's vision, which God gave him after the third captivity.

> The hand of the LORD was on me, and he brought me out by the Spirit of the LORD and set me in the middle of a valley; it was full of bones. He led me back and forth among them, and I saw a great many bones on the floor of the valley, bones that were very dry. He asked me, "Son of man, can these bones live?"
> I said, "Sovereign LORD, you alone know."
> Then he said to me, "Prophesy to these bones and say to them, 'Dry bones, hear the word of the LORD! This is what the Sovereign LORD says to these bones: I will make breath enter you, and you will come to life. I will attach tendons to you and make flesh come upon you and cover you with skin; I will put breath in you, and you will come to life. Then you will know that I am the LORD'"(Ezekiel 37:1-6).

It was like a simultaneous breaking news report. The tears of Jeremiah in Jerusalem and those of Ezekiel in Babylon were flowing at the same time.

About twelve or thirteen years later, God gave the prophet Ezekiel another powerful vision. A man came to him in this dream and told him, "Look carefully and listen closely and pay attention to everything I am going to show you, for that is why you have been brought here. Tell the people of Israel everything you see"(Ezekiel 40:4). God then showed Ezekiel a bird's eye view of the new Jerusalem temple — the measurements of the temple, the exact positions and spaces between the building, the three gates leading into the temple, the rooms for the priest, the inside of the sanctuary. God also showed how His glory would appear in the new temple.

The Vision of Ezekiel
by Francisco Collantes

Here's an example of what Ezekiel observed on the tour of this magnificent structure. "Then he brought me to the inner court on the east side, and he measured the gateway; it had the same measurements as the others. Its alcoves, its projecting walls and its portico had the same measurements as the others. The gateway and its portico had openings all around. It was fifty cubits long and twenty-five cubits wide. Its portico faced the outer court; palm trees decorated the jambs on either side, and eight steps led up to it"(Ezekiel 40:32-34). You can read all the details in the book of Ezekiel starting in Chapter 40.

Ultimately, this vision from God gave new hope. And this is why God said that the seventy years of Babylonian captivity was not solely for punishment, but an avenue that would eventually offer peace and hope for the future. This is an example of how God is love.

Jeremiah's Letter to Babylon

Jeremiah prayed to God all the time. Although he had been falsely accused as being pro-Babylon and treated as a traitor, Jeremiah's heart bled for the people of his nation. And even in the worst of times, his tear-filled prayer was not yet over. "Restore us to yourself, LORD, that we may return; renew our days as of old unless you have utterly rejected us and are angry with us beyond measure"(Lamentations 5:21-22).

Jeremiah took heart and began to write a letter to the people taken captive to Babylon for the purpose of giving hope to those who were living there. The hope was that after seventy years, they would return home. The prophet was diligent in writing this letter, what we know as the book of Jeremiah. He wanted to share of God's infinite mercy and faithfulness and remind them that all was not lost. The written letter eventually reached the hands of Daniel, who was a captive in Babylon. It was through reading Jeremiah's letter that Daniel learned that the Babylonian captivity would last seventy years.

This information is what motivated Daniel to openly live his life in prayer and expect the restoration of Jerusalem. He knelt before God three times a day in his room in defiance of a decree to worship only the king. "Now when Daniel learned that the decree had been published, he went home to his upstairs room where the windows opened toward Jerusalem. Three times a day he got down on his knees and prayed, giving thanks to his God, just as he had done before"(Daniel 6:10).

Babylon's Indoctrination Policy No Match for God's Law

Let's take a look back when, through God's amazing deliverance, the people of Israel left Egypt. After the people arrived at Mount Sinai, they began to intensively study the law of Moses and remained devoted students of the Word of God during the entire forty-year journey to the Promised Land. The law of Moses and the words of the prophets during the

Babylonian captivity provided specific guidelines on how the people of Israel should live. When Jesus came to earth, He confirmed the importance of the law saying, "Do not think that I have come to abolish the Law or the Prophets; I have not come to abolish them but to fulfill them"(Matthew 5:17).

The Babylonian policy mandating that the captives receive intensive education in Babylon's laws and culture was no match for the education the Hebrews received at Mt. Sinai. The Word of God had been instilled in their hearts and minds for generations. Instead of warning about possible indoctrination, Jeremiah advised the Hebrews to make the most of their time in Babylon(see Jeremiah 29:5-7). They were encouraged to live a good life and be a good witness to the people there.

Many leaders rose from the ranks of the captives, leaders who were committed to learning and keeping the laws of God. Young Daniel, for instance, did not associate himself with the ways of Babylon, but kept following God in everything he did; he was promoted within the governments of two empires. After the captivity, other men like Zerubbabel and Nehemiah, who also followed God and were distinguished as excellent leaders, were appointed as governors. Zerubbabel led the first group of captives out of exile, and Nehemiah rebuilt the temple walls.

Jewish Daughters in Babylon
by Herbert Gustave Schmalz

The prophet Ezra, who was born in Babylon, also studied the laws of God. After he returned to Judah, he lived as one of the greatest scholars of the law. "The son of Abishua, the son of Phinehas, the son of Eleazar, the son of Aaron the chief priest — this Ezra came up from Babylon. He was a teacher well versed in the Law of Moses, which the LORD, the God of Israel, had given. The king had granted him everything he asked, for the hand of the LORD his God was on him"(Ezra 7:5-6). Also, a Jewish woman named Esther became the queen of Persia and risked her life to save God's people. (I discuss these individuals in the next chapter).

Simply put, Babylon's efforts to brainwash the young Hebrews into following their laws could not overcome the laws of God.

The Downfall of the Babylonian Empire

Babylon's life span as an empire was just seventy years, the shortest of all empires. Toward the end of the seventy years, the once-feared empire that had conquered the entire ancient Near East including Assyria, Judah, and Egypt was approaching its ruin.

King Nebuchadnezzar, who ruled for forty-three years, was responsible for turning Babylon into a great empire. He exercised a formidable military might and launched massive construction projects. According to Persian tax records, Babylon's economic power amounted to one-third of the whole of Asia. That's a sign of a powerful and strong country.

Issurtar Gate of Babylon
German Pergamon Museum

Nebuchadnezzar was also responsible for turning the city of Babylon into a lavish and exquisitely adorned attraction. According to The Histories of Herodotus, the huge city was located in the middle of a wide plain in the shape of a quadrangle, each side as long as 120 stadion (14 miles or 22.4 km). The Euphrates River flowed through the center of the city. Herodotus also wrote that Babylon was "the most powerful and renowned of them all" and "surpasses in splendour any city of the known world." The city was known for its beauty, particularly its hanging gardens, which became one of the seven wonders of the ancient world.

When King Nebuchadnezzar died, Babylon began her decline. The king's son Amel-marduk ruled for two years before being assassinated by his brother-in-law, Neri-glisser assassinated who then succeeded him on the throne. Labashi-marduk, the son of Neri-glisser, became the next king and was also assassinated not long after he took the throne. Nabonidus, a son of a noble from Haran who was not a family member of Nebuchadnezzar, became the next king and is known to have been the most capable ruler since Nebuchadnezzar.

A conflict arose in the kingdom during the reign of Belshazzar, the son of Nabonidus. (Though the Bible verses below reflect that Belshazzar was Nebuchadnezzar's son, various historical accounts assert that Belshazzar was, in fact, the son of Nabonidus.) Nebuchadnezzar, his family, and the people of Babylon served a god called Marduk while Nabonidus served a god called Sin. During the rule of Belshazzar, Nebuchadnezzar's family and the people of Babylon began to hate Belshazzar and gave their loyalty to Cyrus II of Persia.[25)]

In 538 BC King Belshazzar invited one thousand nobles to attend a party at the palace. The book of Daniel records this event.

> "King Belshazzar gave a great banquet for a thousand of his nobles and drank wine with them. While Belshazzar was drinking his wine, he gave orders to bring in the gold and silver goblets that Nebuchadnezzar his father had taken from the temple in

> Jerusalem, so that the king and his nobles, his wives and his concubines might drink from them. So they brought in the gold goblets that had been taken from the temple of God in Jerusalem, and the king and his nobles, his wives and his concubines drank from them. As they drank the wine, they praised the gods of gold and silver, of bronze, iron, wood and stone"(Daniel 5:1-4).

In the midst of the partying, "suddenly the fingers of a human hand appeared and wrote on the plaster of the wall, near the lampstand in the royal palace. The king watched the hand as it wrote"(Daniel 5:5). Can you imagine how frightened the king and all his guests were? The Bible tells us that the king's face turned pale and his knees started knocking(see verse 6).

King Belshazzar called in all the astrologers and wise men of Babylon and asked them to interpret the writing on the wall. He promised that whoever could tell him its meaning would be "clothed in purple and have a gold chain placed around his neck, and he will be made the third highest ruler in the kingdom"(see verse 7). Nevertheless, nobody could interpret the

Belshazzar's Banquet
by Rembrandt

writing on the wall(see verse 8).

Then the queen remembered Daniel and how years before he had told King Nebuchadnezzar his dream and interpreted it for him. She told King Belshazzar, "There is a man in your kingdom who has the spirit of the holy gods in him. In the time of your father he was found to have insight and intelligence and wisdom like that of the gods. Your father, King Nebuchadnezzar, appointed him chief of the magicians, enchanters, astrologers and diviners. He did this because Daniel, whom the king called Belteshazzar, was found to have a keen mind and knowledge and understanding, and also the ability to interpret dreams, explain riddles and solve difficult problems. Call for Daniel, and he will tell you what the writing means"(Daniel 5:11-12).

Daniel came in and explained to the king the writing on the wall.

> This is the inscription that was written:
> MENE, MENE, TEKEL, PARSIN.
> "Here is what these words mean:
> *Mene:* God has numbered the days of your reign and brought it to an end.
> *Tekel:* You have been weighed on the scales and found wanting.
> *Peres:* Your kingdom is divided and given to the Medes and Persians."
> (Daniel 5:25-28)

Although the writing on the wall indicated that Belshazzar's kingdom was over, the king fulfilled his promise. "Then at Belshazzar's command, Daniel was clothed in purple, a gold chain was placed around his neck, and he was proclaimed the third highest ruler in the kingdom. That very night Belshazzar, king of the Babylonians, was slain, and Darius the Mede took over the kingdom, at the age of sixty-two"(Daniel 5:29-30).

Cylinder describing Repairs on the Temple of the Moon-god Sin at Ur
by King Nabonidus, with a Prayer for his Son Belshazzar
(The British Museum)

That night, Babylon was destroyed by Persia. The Persian army invaded the city of Babylon without a fight. During the feast of Belshazzar, the Babylonians had just been defeated at the Battle of Opis. Armed with that victory, the Persian army simply walked into the city victorious against the empire.

God's Management of the Universe

The keyword I connect to the way Babylon managed its empire is "education." They used education to conquer other nations and advance the Babylonian agenda. Education is a long-term policy. It's ironic that, with education at the center of its imperial policy, the Babylonian empire didn't even last that long. Surviving just seventy years, Babylon had the shortest reign of all the empires of the world.

God also considers education to be the most important way to further his message. Daniel was one of God's key players in teaching the law to His people. King Nebuchadnezzar, however, planned to educate Daniel in the ways of Babylon, make him a faithful subject of his empire, and use him to rule other nations under the flag of the Babylonian Empire. But God thought otherwise.

No powerful group, nation, or empire can achieve absolute control over the world, not even with a well-designed education strategy. This is because God intended our education to give us understanding into who we are, not as a force to control others.

CHAPTER 3
BIBLE with PERSIAN EMPIRE

The books of the Bible related to Persia

Daniel, Haggai, Zechariah, Esther, Ezra,
Nehemiah,Malachi, II Chronicles etc.

The Persian Empire and the Seven Books of the Old Testament

Persia is the ancient name of modern day Iran. It is related to seven of the thirty-nine books of the Old Testament (Daniel, Haggai, Zechariah, Esther, Ezra, Nehemiah, and Malachi). The book of Daniel is connected to the Persian Empire because of Daniel's involvement with the government. The prophets Haggai and Zechariah, active during the time of the Persian Empire, urged the people of Israel to rebuild the temple of Jerusalem that was destroyed by the Babylonians. The book of Esther tells us the story of the Jewish woman who became the queen of Persia and res-

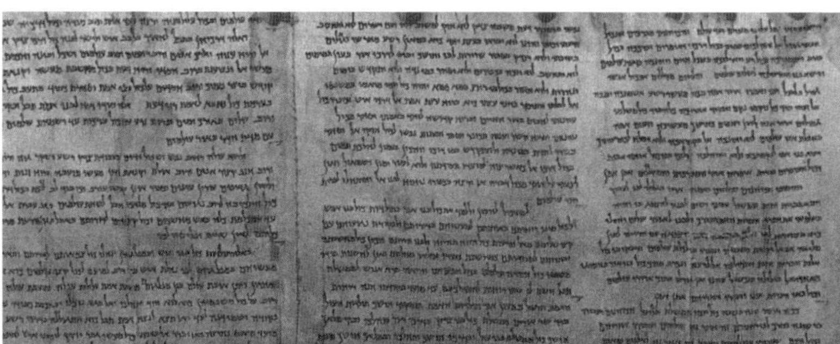

The Dead Sea Scrolls

cued the nation of Israel from annihilation; this occurred between the first and second captivities, although historian Flavius Josephus claims this event occurred after the Hebrews returned from the third captivity. Ezra, the scholar, led the second return of the captives, and Nehemiah, a governor and cupbearer to the king, was the leader of the third return. Finally, in the book of Malachi, the last book of the Old Testament, we are told a story about a governor who is dispatched by Persia.

Pharaoh of Egypt and Cyrus the Great

I want to briefly compare the Pharaoh of Egypt, who ruled during the time of Moses, to the first king of Persia, Cyrus II, commonly known as Cyrus the Great. Pharaoh was at the epicenter of the Israelite's exodus out of Egypt, and King Cyrus II with their exodus out of Babylon. I consider these two events the cornerstones of the Old Testament.

These two leaders treated the Israelites very differently. King Cyrus II looked upon God's people with favor, while Pharaoh's heart was closed to their plight. The Bible says, "But the LORD hardened Pharaoh's heart and he would not listen to Moses and Aaron, just as the LORD had said to Moses"(Exodus 9:12). King Cyrus II, however, was more receptive to the

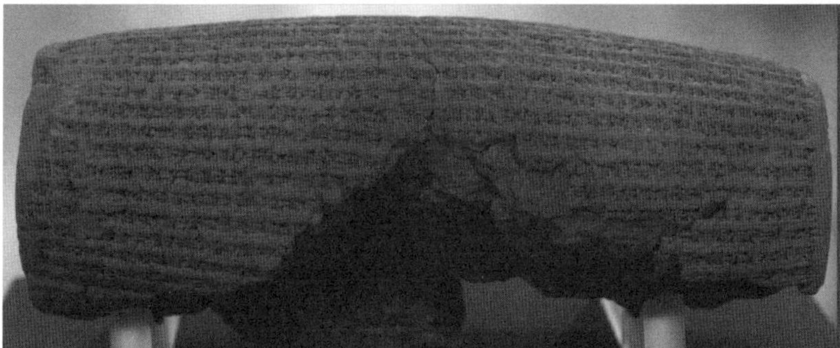

The Cyrus Cylinder
The British Museum

words of the prophets. "In the first year of Cyrus king of Persia, in order to fulfill the word of the LORD spoken by Jeremiah, the LORD moved the heart of Cyrus king of Persia to make a proclamation throughout his realm and also to put it in writing"(Ezra 1:1).

Pharaoh was a cruel, unyielding leader who wouldn't allow the Hebrew people to leave Egypt. He said to Moses, "Who is the LORD, that I should obey him and let Israel go? I do not know the LORD and I will not let Israel go"(Exodus 5:2). Cyrus the Great was a great king who was called "father" by his people.[26] The first chapter of Ezra tells us how he allowed the captive Hebrews to return to their homeland.

King of Persia, King of Lydia, and Solon the Greek Sage

Before the existence of the Persian Empire, ancient Persia and Media were kingdoms in what is known today as Iran. Astyages, the king of Media who ruled from 585 to 550 BC, had a daughter named Mandane. According to the Greek historian Herodotus, shortly after her birth, the king had a strange dream in which his daughter urinated so much she flooded all of Asia. King Astyages asked the Magi, or wise priests, to interpret the dream. (It seems to me that when the likes of Kings Pharaoh and Nebuchadnezzar dream, distress always follows.)

Much to his alarm, the priests told the king that Mandane's son would overthrow the king and eventually occupy all of Asia. Because of this foreboding, King Astyages did not choose a Median husband for his daughter when the time came, but opted to marry her off to Cambyses, a Persian man who posed no threat to him.

After Mandane became pregnant, the king had another dream, one more outrageous than the first. He was so frightened by it, he ordered his right hand man, Harpagus, to kill his grandson, Cyrus II, upon birth. Harpagus did not obey the king, however, and entrusted the baby boy to a farmer-couple who were tending cows in the mountains.

At the same time, a son also was born to the couple but sadly died at birth. While making the funeral arrangements, the wife switched the babies' identities so that everyone believed it was the princess's son who had died. Upon hearing the (false) news that their baby boy had died, Mandane and Cambyses moved to Persia and spent the rest of their days there.

The farmer-couple raised the royal baby as their own flesh and blood. But when Cyrus II was ten years old, something strange happened. He started playing "king" with a group of children and had them act out roles in his make-believe kingdom. He even ordered the children to report to him if they saw a child violating his orders. When the future king was notified of one particular "subject's" disobedience, he flogged the little boy. The father of the child that Cyrus II punished was a noble in Media. He was enraged by the incident and told King Astyages what had happened. The king was troubled by the story and went to visit the boy. King Astyages immediately recognized his grandson and sent him to Persia where his birth parents lived.

King Astyages refused to forgive Harpagus for his betrayal and plotted a barbaric revenge. He had one of Harpagus's sons killed and later, invited

The World's First Gold Coin, the Lydian Lion

Harpagus to join him in a meal where he served the flesh of the dead young man.

Harpagus then harbored a deep-seeded grudge and began scheming of a way to use the king's own grandson to plot a revolt against him. Harpagus was a driving force in causing the Persians to turn against King Astyages. He also played a vital part in Cyrus II's ascension to the Persian throne.

Now King of Persia, Cyrus II and Harpagus led battles against Media. When Cyrus II advanced to the capital of Ecbatana and occupied the city in 550 BC, King Astyages' dream was eerily starting to come to pass. He was dethroned, and Cyrus II combined Persia and Media and ruled over the combined territory. He rapidly began to expand what became known as the Persian Empire. In his twenty-nine year reign, the king conquered Lydia, Assyria, Babylon, Bactria, Sogdiana, and Asia, thereby creating the biggest empire to date.

Before King Cyrus II became king, Persia was very poor; the city had no trade of any kind. On the other hand, Lydia, known today as Turkey, had tremendous riches. King Cyrus II's conquest of Lydia is how Persia acquired most of her wealth. (In much the same way, Lydia's king, Croesus, was the first king to conquer Greece and receive her tribute.[27])

In 547 BC, King Cyrus II attacked Sardis, the capital of Lydia, and occupied it in two weeks.[28] King Croesus was captured and prepared for execution. He was placed on a pyre and about to be burned when he started muttering to himself. King Cyrus II wanted to know what he was saying and sent for an interpreter.

Croesus on the Pyre, Attic Red Figure Amphora, 500-490 BC Louvre Museum

The man reported that King Croesus was looking for Solon, one of the seven wise men of Greece. This mystery intrigued the Persian king, and in that moment he decided not to execute the Lydian.

King Cyrus II directed that King Croesus be taken down from the pyre, but it was already on fire. Suddenly it began to rain and the fire was put out instantly. Thinking that heaven must have stopped Croesus from burning alive, King Cyrus II started conversing with the king of Lydia. The two men shared an interesting and deep discussion about a man's true happiness and other philosophical matters.

King Croesus told Cyrus II that he had encountered Solon when the wise man was traveling around the world and came to visit Lydia. The king, who was the wealthiest man in the ancient Near East and gave the largest of all offerings to the Greek gods, asked the sage who was the "happiest person" he had ever met. Croesus, of course, wanted Solon to say that the king was the happiest. Solon's answer, however, was not the response the king was looking for.

The sage told him two stories, one of a man named Tellus, who died for his country on the battlefield, and another of two brothers, Cleobis and Bito, who died peacefully in their sleep. Croesus was astonished that Solon did not point to the king as being the happiest in light of his tremendous wealth. But that was the wise man's point. Riches did not equate happiness.

The Relics of Persia
The British Museum

When Croesus was on the edge of death, he realized the value of what Solon had said. Upon hearing this story, King Cyrus II was also deeply moved and inspired to reflect. He became friends with Croesus and even appointed him as an advisor in his kingdom. Later, when King Cyrus II was detailing his will to his son Cambyses II, he told his son to treat Croesus with respect for the rest of his life.

After his dramatic and merciful rescue from the pyre, King Croesus heard reports that Persian soldiers were pillaging the city of Lydia. He asked King Cyrus II why he allowed his soldiers to destroy the conquered city when all that wealth now belonged to the king. The Lydian king's wise guidance prompted King Cyrus II to order the soldiers to stop. On that day, the Persian king acquired the wealth of Lydia and eventually built a considerable army, which paved the way toward creating a massive empire.

Cyrus the Great, the Father of Persia

The Bible testifies that "...in order to fulfill the word of the LORD spoken by Jeremiah"(Ezra 1:1), God moved the heart of King Cyrus II. In 537 BC, the king allowed the captives of Judah who were taken to Babylon to return to their homeland.

Just as there were three captivities, the return of the Jewish people took place on three separate occasions. The Jewish leader Zerubbabel (I'll talk more about him in the next few pages) led the first return in 537 BC; the priest Ezra led the second in 458 BC, and Nehemiah led the third in 445 BC.

King Cyrus II was a friend to the Jews. Not only did he orchestrate their official release, but he also issued a proclamation that allowed the Jewish people to rebuild the temple in Jerusalem that had been previously destroyed. "In the first year of Cyrus king of Persia, in order to fulfill the word of the Lord spoken by Jeremiah, the Lord moved the heart of Cyrus

The Tomb of Cyrus the Great
Pasargadae, Iran

king of Persia to make a proclamation throughout his realm and also to put it in writing: "This is what Cyrus king of Persia says: "'The LORD, the God of heaven, has given me all the kingdoms of the earth and he has appointed me to build a temple for him at Jerusalem in Judah"(Ezra 1:1-2). (In the above passage, the "first year of Cyrus" does not mean the first year of his rule as king, but refers to the year the Persian Empire completed the conquest of Babylon and began the Persian rule.)

King Cyrus II also allowed the people who wished to remain in Persia the opportunity to give monies and offering to Jerusalem. We discover later in history that these people were known as the Jewish Diaspora, Jews who did not live in their homeland but visited Jerusalem at least once a year on the days of the feasts and gave tithes to the temple. They were also encouraged to contribute to the Jerusalem's economy through consumerism.

As a side note, the word "Jew" was first used in Babylon. The Babylonians classified the people taken captive from the kingdom of Judah as Jews because they were from the tribes of Judah and Benjamin. In Egypt, the descendants of Abraham were called Hebrews. As these people were coming out of Egypt, they called themselves Israel. When the north and south split, the people of the Northern Kingdom of Israel were called Samaritans, a group of people with mixed races.

In *The Works of Flavius Josephus* we find how many Jews returned from Persia under the rule of King Cyrus II. "But the sum of those that went up, above the age of twelve years, of the tribes of Judah and Benjamin, was four hundred and sixty-two myriads and eight thousand, the Levites were seventy-four; the number of the women and children, mixed together, was forty thousand seven hundred and forty-two; and besides these, there were singers of the Levites one hundred and twenty-eight, and porters one hundred and ten, and of the sacred ministers three hundred and ninety-two; there were also others besides these, who said they were of the Israelites, but were notable to show their genealogies, six hundred and sixty-two."[29] This source also records there were many others who did not return to Judah but offered much money for the rebuilding of the temple.

In the second chapter of Ezra, we read that the returnees numbered 42,360(see Ezra 2:64). Among those, there were 7,337 servants, 200 male and female singers, 736 horses, 245 mules, 435 camels, and 6,720 donkeys(see Ezra 2:65-67).

The Rise of King Darius

When King Cyrus II died, his son Cambyses II became the second king of Persia and ruled for almost eight years (530-522 BC). While the people affectionately referred to his father as the empire's father, Cambyses II was called a tyrant.

King Cambyses II married his two sisters, Atossa (who later became the queen of King Darius) and Meroe. He killed Meroe when he heard her mourning the death of their brother, Smerdis, whom the king ordered to be killed in 525 BC.

Cambyses II's Symbol

When King Cambyses II was in Egypt, following a successful invasion of the country, he heard surprising news that Smerdis was reigning as king in the Persian capital of Susa. King Cambyses II called in his subject Pracsaspes, whom he had ordered to kill his brother, and questioned him about the disturbing report. Pracsaspes confirmed he had killed Smerdis with his own hands.[30] If that was true, then the man acting as king must have been a fake. King Cambyses II decided to go to Persia to investigate, but he died as he mounted his horse.[31]

As it turned out, the king of Susa happened to have the same name as King Cambyses II's deceased brother, and he even looked like him. King Smerdis used these similarities to his advantage and pretended to be King Cyrus' son. However, Smerdis did not rule like a real king. He didn't make any public appearances and kept hidden in the palace. A man by the name of Otanes became suspicious of these peculiarities.

Otanes was a Persian noble whose daughter was married to Smerdis. She confessed to her father Smerdis' true identity, that he was not the son of King Cyrus II. Otanes told some friends, and they plotted to dethrone him. Darius, who was the governor of Persia, arrived in Susa around this time and joined the group of conspirators. It wasn't easy for the group of seven men to plot a revolt and dethrone Smerdis because the Magi and his older brother, a Median priest, in particular, devoutly defended him.

When Pracsaspes arrived from Egypt, the priest convinced him to tell the people of Susa that Smerdis was the real son of King Cyrus II. Instead, on the day of the announcement, with many people gathered around the palace, Pracsaspes told the crowd that Smerdis was in fact a fraud and that he himself had killed the real Smerdis. Pracsaspes then committed suicide by throwing himself over the palace walls. Seeing this as the perfect opportunity to implement their plan, Otanes and the six other conspirators marched into the palace and killed Smerdis and the Magi.

The incident came to be called the Slaughter of the Magi and was recognized as a national annual holiday. Every year on that day, priests were forbidden to leave their house. If they were seen wandering the streets, they could be killed. In the days of Queen Esther, as recorded in the Bible, Haman, a Persian noble, attempted to create a similar holiday out of his evil desire to annihilate the Jewish people.

Since Persia was without a king, the seven conspirators discussed the leadership of the country. They decided to compete for the throne, with the exception of Otanes, who was exempt from the political race and was instead granted special privileges for him and his family.

The winner of the crown would be decided on the outcome of a horse race. The one whose horse made the first sound after the race would be king. One of Darius's servants was an excellent rider and helped him in this competition. The night before the race, the servant mated Darius's horse with a female horse and sprinkled the urine of the female horse at the finishing line. When the competitors finished the race, Darius's horse cried out when it smelled the urine, and Darius won. He became king of Persia and ruled from 521 to 486 BC. Darius had the following inscribed on his epitaph: "Darius, son of Hystapses, by the virtue of his horse and of his groom Oebares, won the throne of Persia."[32]

The Persian Governor Zerubbabel

Though he was Jewish, Zerubbabel, the leader of the first release of the Babylonian captives, was appointed by both Kings Cyrus II and Darius to the position of governor. At that time, a governor was akin to being second in command. Although there were perhaps Persian officials who were qualified for the job, the kings took notice of Zerubbabel and gave him power.

Flavius Josephus recorded an important episode concerning Zerubbabel and King Darius. According to Josephus the two men had been friends for a long time, even before Darius sat on the throne. Darius swore to his friend that if he became king, he would rebuild the temple in Jerusalem and return all the articles of God to it.[33]

When Darius became the third king of Persia, Zerubbabel was made the governor of the Jews; he was also assigned as a bodyguard to the king. One day, the king threw a big party to which he invited his inner circle, nobles from other countries, and various military commanders. When the party was over and Darius went to bed, he had trouble sleeping.

The king called in three of his guards including Zerubbabel and posed to them a question. He told them that the one who gave the wisest answer would be given, among other opulent gifts, purple clothes, a gold bed, and a gold chain to wear around his neck. Darius asked the guards what was the strongest on earth — a king, a woman, alcohol, or truth. He then told them to think about the question and return to him the next day with their answer.

The one who answered correctly was Zerubbabel. He reasoned that although a king, a woman, and alcohol are certainly strong, all of these things are under the control of God, who is Truth. Therefore, Zerubbabel said, since all things are temporal, it is most important to follow Truth because it is eternal and will never change.

Darius the Great
National Museum of Iran

Darius accepted Zerubbabel's answer and told him he would grant him any wish. Zerubbabel said he would like the king to keep the promise he made to him years before he become king. Darius was pleased and accepted his friend's wish. He vowed to have the temple of

Jerusalem rebuilt and all the articles of the temple returned to their proper place. In the second year of his reign, Darius found a decree written by King Cyrus II the promise to rebuild the destroyed temple. And to the great joy of the Jewish people, he restarted construction of the temple as the king had intended to do.[34]

> "King Darius then issued an order, and they searched in the archives stored in the treasury at Babylon. A scroll was found in the citadel of Ecbatana in the province of Media, and this was written on it: Memorandum: In the first year of King Cyrus, the king issued a decree concerning the temple of God in Jerusalem: Let the temple be rebuilt as a place to present sacrifices, and let its foundations be laid. It is to be sixty cubits high and sixty cubits wide, with three courses of large stones and one of timbers. The costs are to be paid by the royal treasury"(Ezra 6:1-4).

Under the order of King Cyrus II, the first group of returnees began rebuilding the foundation of the temple, but they did not complete the

Archers Frieze from Darius' Palace at Susa
Louvre Museum

project. The Samaritans found out about the construction and wanted to be involved in the work. At that time, there was much conflict between the Jews and the Samaritans, and both groups discouraged contact with the other. Though the Samaritans offered help, the Jews refused it, wanting to carry out the work with only Jewish workers. The conflict temporarily disrupted the project until it was resumed under

King Darius.

Finally, in 516 BC the very temple of Jerusalem that had been severely destroyed was taking shape, although it was smaller and less opulent than the temple of Solomon's time. When Herod the Great ruled many years later, he began an extension of the temple, which is called the Third Temple.

After ruling for thirty-six years, King Darius died in 486 BC. Some of his important historical moments include the Battle of Marathon, when he intended to occupy Greece but returned defeated, and his efforts trying to subdue the Egypt rebellion right before his death. Darius's son Xerxes, the next and fourth king of Persia, is introduced to us in the Biblical book of Esther.

Queen Esther and King Xerxes

The book of Esther begins, "This is what happened during the time of Xerxes, the Xerxes who ruled over 127 provinces stretching from India to Cush"(Esther 1:1). During the third year of his rule the Persian king Xerxes hosted a banquet in order to show off his riches. It lasted one hundred and eighty days. Xerxes also wanted to display his beautiful queen, Queen Vashti, to his guests, so he ordered her to be brought before him. The queen, however, rejected her husband's request.

> "On the seventh day, when King Xerxes was in high spirits from wine, he commanded the seven eunuchs who served him — Mehuman, Biztha, Harbona, Bigtha, Abagtha, Zethar and Karkas — to bring before him Queen Vashti, wearing her royal crown, in order to display her beauty to the people and nobles, for she was lovely to look at. But when the attendants delivered

Xerxes, Haman, Esther
by Rembrandt

the king's command, Queen Vashti refused to come. Then the king became furious and burned with anger"(Esther 1:10-12).

According to *The Works of Flavius Josephus*, a Chaldee paraphrast, or interpreter, remarked that the king intended to show his guests the queen's naked body. If this is true, we can see why she wouldn't oblige her husband's request. Also, the Bible tells us that the king was "high in spirits"(see Esther 1:10) so perhaps he did this because he was drunk. Whatever the reason, the king felt insulted by his wife. He asked his advisors for help interpreting the law about how wives should respect their husbands. Concluding that the queen was disrespectful, the wise men recommended that King Xerxes drive Queen Vashti out of the palace and find himself a new queen.

The second chapter of the Old Testament book tells us how the Jewish woman Esther came on the scene.

"The king's personal attendants proposed, "Let a search be made for beautiful young virgins for the king. Let the king appoint commissioners in every province of his realm to bring all these beau-

> tiful young women into the harem at the citadel of Susa. Let them be placed under the care of Hegai, the king's eunuch, who is in charge of the women; and let beauty treatments be given to them. Then let the young woman who pleases the king be queen instead of Vashti." This advice appealed to the king, and he followed it. Now there was in the citadel of Susa a Jew of the tribe of Benjamin, named Mordecai son of Jair, the son of Shimei, the son of Kish, who had been carried into exile from Jerusalem by Nebuchadnezzar king of Babylon, among those taken captive with Jehoiachin king of Judah. Mordecai had a cousin named Hadassah, whom he had brought up because she had neither father nor mother. This young woman, who was also known as Esther, had a lovely figure and was beautiful. Mordecai had taken her as his own daughter when her father and mother died"(Esther 2:2-7).

After a yearlong beauty preparation, Esther was selected as the most attractive woman. She became the queen during the seventh year of King Xerxes's rule, after he had returned from an unsuccessful four-year expedition to conquer Greece.[35)]

In those days, there was a great conflict between Mordecai, Esther's uncle, and Haman, a Persian noble and vizier under the king. The hostility concerned Haman's desire to obliterate the Jewish people. According to Flavius Josephus, Haman was a descendent of the Amalekites, who had been totally destroyed by the Jews, and he held a grudge against the people of Judah.[36)] Haman convinced the king to enact a decree to kill all Jews and plunder their personal property and possessions.

> "Dispatches were sent by couriers to all the king's provinces with the order to destroy, kill and annihilate all the Jews — young and old, women and children — on a single day, the thirteenth day

> of the twelfth month, the month of Adar, and to plunder their goods. A copy of the text of the edict was to be issued as law in every province and made known to the people of every nationality so they would be ready for that day.
> The couriers went out, spurred on by the king's command, and the edict was issued in the citadel of Susa. The king and Haman sat down to drink, but the city of Susa was bewildered"(Esther 3:13-15).

Because Esther was a Jew, unbeknownst to the king, she was upset by this decree and was determined to resolve the matter by going to her husband, even if it meant risking her very life. She asked Mordecai for support, "Go, gather together all the Jews who are in Susa, and fast for me. Do not eat or drink for three days, night or day. I and my maids will fast as you do. When this is done, I will go to the king, even though it is against the law. And if I perish, I perish"(Esther 4:16). Through a series of interesting conversations and events, Esther's great wisdom, and the Lord's intervention for His people, the decree was withdrawn. The Jewish population was spared from death.

The avoided catastrophe called for a holiday, and Mordecai established the annual feast of Purim. "Mordecai recorded these events, and he sent letters to all the Jews throughout the provinces of King Xerxes, near and far, to have them celebrate annually the fourteenth and fifteenth days of the month of Adar as the time when the Jews got relief from their enemies, and as the month when their sorrow was turned into joy and their mourning into a day of celebration. He wrote them to observe the days as days of feasting and joy and giving presents of food to one another and gifts to the poor"(Esther 9:20-22).

King Xerxes Recorded in World History

The Xerxes mentioned in the Bible, who showed compassion on the Jewish people as told in the book of Esther, and the one mentioned in world history seem like two different people. Some depict him as a cruel king, as shown in the movie 300 in the battle between Persia and Leonidas of Sparta and his three hundred men. This, however, is up for debate.

Before Darius became king, he had already married and had three children. After he became king, he married Atossa, the daughter of King Cyrus II, and together they had four more children. Xerxes was their first son. When Xerxes became king of Persia after his father, he was given the task of conquering Greece, something his father failed to do when he suffered defeat during the Battle of Marathon.

When Xerxes ruled Persia, the largest empire of the world, his territory reached as far as Pakistan today to the east, as far as central and west Asia to the west, as far as Macedonia to the north, and as far as Sinai Peninsula and Egypt, making it almost as big as North America.

While Xerxes first intended to conquer Egypt, his cousin and brother-in-law who was also a member of his inner circle, persuaded him to conquer Greece instead. Xerxes took his advice and left for the Greek expedition. He took with him 700,000 soldiers from various countries.[37] Because these soldiers spoke different languages, I imagine it must have been a challenge to give them orders.

Greece had already begun making preparations to defend against the inevitable second invasion of Persia. Although they had been victorious against King Darius in the Battle of Marathon, a victory against his son, Xerxes was not guaranteed.

Before the second battle took place, a silver mine was discovered in

Sea Battle at Salamis
by Wilhelm von Kaulbach

the Greek town of Laurium.[38] The general consensus was to distribute some of the riches to the citizens of Athens, but a politician named Themistocles had another idea. He proposed they build two hundred ships and build up Greece's navy. He figured they had a better chance of winning the war against Persia on water than on land. The proposition was accepted and the navy was strengthened.

When King Xerxes attacked, Greece won a great victory by drawing Xerxes into Salamis, an island in the Saronic Gulf. The Battle of Salamis, an eight-hour battle in which over two hundred thousand soldiers from Africa, Asia, and Europe fought,[39] was one of the greatest naval battles in the world.[40] A fleet of three hundred and eighty ships from the Greek allied forces fought against a fleet of about nine hundred Persian ships. Before this monumental battle, according to Barry Strauss, author of *The Battle of Salamis*, Persia had already lost about four hundred battleships in a monster typhoon.[41]

Although Persia was tremendously defeated in this war, the Battle of Salamis is only briefly mentioned in its history. (If you look at historical accounts of war, defeated armies have a habit of not including the battles they lost as part of their records.) Persia's losing streak continued. The following year King Xerxes lost the Battle of Plataea against Greece. And with the loss of yet another conflict at the Battle of Mycale, Persia withdrew from Greece.

Ezra and the Second Return of the Captives

When King Xerxes was murdered in 465 BC, his son, Artaxerxes, took the throne and ruled until 423 BC. According to Flavius Josephus, this king "inherited not only his father's throne but also a godly mind of faith in God."[42] Artaxerxes helped facilitate the return of the second group of captives at the persuasions of Ezra, a highly respected Jewish priest and scribe.

Born in Babylon where his parents were taken captive, Ezra was extremely knowledgeable(see Ezra 7:6) and became an advisor to King Artaxerxes. When Ezra expressed to the king his desire to return to Jerusalem, the king fully supported his wish. In 458 BC, Ezra led the return of the second group of captives. After arriving in Jerusalem, he "devoted himself to the study and observance of the Law of the LORD, and to teaching its decrees and laws in Israel"(Ezra 7:10). He also led a passionate campaign to purify the Jewish community by, among other things, discouraging mixed marriages.

The Tomb of Artaxerxes at Naqsh-e Rustam

In the seventh chapter of the book of Ezra, we see an abstract of the decree given by King Artaxerxes to Ezra. This official document, authorized by the king, permitted the captives who remained in Persia to return to Judah. This proclamation also included instructions on how the returnees should conduct their lives at home. Though it may be a bit lengthy, I find the text impressive and fascinating.

> "Artaxerxes, king of kings, To Ezra the priest, teacher of the Law of the God of heaven: Greetings.
> Now I decree that any of the Israelites in my kingdom, including priests and Levites, who volunteer to go to Jerusalem with you, may go. You are sent by the king and his seven advisers to inquire about Judah and Jerusalem with regard to the Law of your God, which is in your hand. Moreover, you are to take with you the silver and gold that the king and his advisers have freely given to the God of Israel, whose dwelling is in Jerusalem, together with all the silver and gold you may obtain from the province of Babylon, as well as the freewill offerings of the people and priests for the temple of their God in Jerusalem. With this money be sure to buy bulls, rams and male lambs, together with their grain offerings and drink offerings, and sacrifice them on the altar of the temple of your God in Jerusalem.
> You and your fellow Israelites may then do whatever seems best with the rest of the silver and gold, in accordance with the will of your God. Deliver to the God of Jerusalem all the articles entrusted to you for worship in the temple of your God. And anything else needed for the temple of your God that you are responsible to supply, you may provide from the royal treasury.
> Now I, King Artaxerxes, decree that all the treasurers of Trans-Euphrates are to provide with diligence whatever Ezra the priest, the teacher of the Law of the God of heaven, may ask of you — up to a hundred talents of silver, a hundred cors of wheat, a hun-

dred baths of wine, a hundred baths of olive oil, and salt without limit. Whatever the God of heaven has prescribed, let it be done with diligence for the temple of the God of heaven. Why should his wrath fall on the realm of the king and of his sons? You are also to know that you have no authority to impose taxes, tribute or duty on any of the priests, Levites, musicians, gatekeepers, temple servants or other workers at this house of God.

And you, Ezra, in accordance with the wisdom of your God, which you possess, appoint magistrates and judges to administer justice to all the people of Trans-Euphrates — all who know the laws of your God. And you are to teach any who do not know them. Whoever does not obey the law of your God and the law of the king must surely be punished by death, banishment, confiscation of property, or imprisonment"(Ezra 7:12-26).

Nehemiah and the Third Return of the Captives

Ezra wasn't the only prophet who had a personal connection with King Artaxerxes. Nehemiah became a cupbearer to the king and was later appointed by him as the governor of Jerusalem.

Cupbearers are frequently mentioned in the Old Testament, and many of the prophets I have mentioned held that position. Today, one might think of a cupbearer as a meaningless or lowly position, but in ancient times, it was a high-ranking and important function within the government. When Joseph was

A Silver Glass with Gold Pattern_ The British Museum

Nehemiah Makes his Petition to Artaxerxes
by William Brassey Hole

in prison in Egypt, he shared a cell with the king's cupbearer. The cupbearer was eventually released from prison and placed in his previous role. "He restored the chief cupbearer to his position, so that he once again put the cup into Pharaoh's hand"(Genesis 40:21). This statement indicates a cupbearer served the king face to face, which denotes a personal and close relationship.

During Nehemiah's service as a cupbearer to King Artaxerxes, Nehemiah's brother and other men returned from a visit to Jerusalem. They relayed to him the horrible conditions of the city of Jerusalem. It had been one hundred and fifty years since the city fell at the hands of the Babylonians, and it was still in disarray. "Hanani, one of my brothers, came from Judah with some other men, and I questioned them about the Jewish remnant that had survived the exile, and also about Jerusalem. They said to me, "Those who survived the exile and are back in the province are in great trouble and disgrace. The wall of Jerusalem is broken down, and its gates have been burned with fire"(Nehemiah 1:2-3). Nehemiah was heartbroken and was determined to rectify the situation and rebuild the walls of Jerusalem.

The king noticed a drastic change in the cupbearer's disposition(see Nehemiah 2:1-2). He asked him what was troubling him, and Nehemiah told him of his desire to go back to Judah and rebuild the walls of Jerusalem. His wish was granted. "Then the king, with the queen sitting beside him, asked me, "How long will your journey take, and when will you get back?" It pleased the king to send me; so I set a time"(Nehemiah 2:5-6).

Nehemiah Views the Ruins of Jerusalem's Walls
by Gustave Dore

This conversation evidences the deep trust the king had in Nehemiah and how the Judean served him faithfully. We also see how important his job as a cupbearer was, as the king and queen asked when he would return. Nehemiah was of great value to the king because he had integrity and a reputable character. Talented people are a dime a dozen, but finding someone who is trustworthy is not always an easy task.

Nehemiah asked the king for certain things to fulfill his desire to which the king gave him everything he needed. "I also said to him, "If it pleases the king, may I have letters to the governors of Trans-Euphrates, so that they will provide me safe-conduct until I arrive in Judah? And may I have a letter to Asaph, keeper of the royal park, so he will give me timber to make beams for the gates of the citadel by the temple and for the city wall and for the residence I will occupy?" And because the gracious hand of my God was on me, the king granted my request"(Nehemiah 2:7-8).

Besides being a cupbearer, Nehemiah also had superior administration skills. He returned to Jerusalem as the appointed governor and oversaw the rebuilding the Jerusalem wall in fifty-two days(see Nehemiah 6:15). Nehemiah is just one example of the many skilled and intelligent captive Jews that Jeremiah foresaw returning to Jerusalem. These same captives from Judah did not fall back into their old ways, following after idols and the ways of the world instead of God, after leaving Persia; they followed the laws of God.

The Downfall of the Persian Empire

When King Artaxerxes died, his son Xerxes II succeeded him. Several other kings subsequently had their turn at the crown before Artaxerxes III came into power in 358 BC. King Artaxerxes III had a terrible reputation for being bloodthirsty. His reign ended tragically when Bagoas, a powerful vizier, murdered the king and most of his family. His son Arses, one of the few survivors, ascended to the throne. Amidst the large number of palace struggles and assassinations, the downfall of the empire was eminent.

During the reign of Darius III, who was the last king of Persia, King Alexander of Macedonia, also known as Alexander the Great, attacked the empire in the Battle of Issus (333 BC). King Darius III had amassed a huge army, increasing the number of Persian soldiers from three hundred twelve thousand to six hundred thousand, but he still suffered defeat. Some records indicate that one hundred thousand Persian foot soldiers and ten

The mosaic representing the battle of Alexander the Great against Darius III, perhaps after an earlier Greek paining of Philoxenus of Eretria. It was found in Pompeii in the House of the Faun and is now in the National Archeological Museum of Naples.

thousand cavalrymen were killed or imprisoned.[43)] This battle signaled the end of the Persian Empire, And after ruling for two hundred and six years, she closed her doors. The Hellenistic Empire, led by Alexander the Great, was right on Persia's heels.

God's Management of the Universe

I associate the word "numbers" with the management of the Persian Empire. Generally speaking, numbers are what determine an empire's power — the size of a territory, how many people live there, how big the army is. When Persia first came into being, she was a poor country without a free market. When King Cyrus II ruled, however, he strengthened the nation so that it had a strong economy; all the kings who ruled the empire were extremely rich. King Cyrus II, however, was not just known for his wealth; he was a significant influence in the lives of the Jewish people. And unlike the ideologies of the Assyrians and Babylonians, this king expanded the Persian Empire with generosity and wisdom.

The Persian Empire had always been confident of its large number of soldiers in their army. During his reign, King Darius took an army of three to four hundred thousand soldiers with him to occupy Greece. Though he failed at the task, it didn't stop the empire from amassing a fortune. We must not forget the vastness of the territory accumulated under Persia's reign. At the height of its empire, she was as big as about 8 million kilometers, spanning Asia, Africa, and Europe.

The power, strength, economic stability, and defense of countries or empires do not depend on numbers; they depend on and are in the hands of God. Many people believe that having a large number of something — whether money, property, a following of people — automatically gives you power and control. Not according to God.

In God's view, one person armed with His power and might is more powerful than a large army. In God's economy, it's not the size that counts; it matters only if God is in the midst. It's just like He told the people of Israel. If they followed after Him and kept His commandments, they would pursue and overtake their enemies, even in small numbers. "Five of you will chase a hundred, and a hundred of you will chase ten thousand, and your enemies will fall by the sword before you" (Leviticus 26:8). Though Persia believed she was strong, powerful, and mighty and depended on her size and "bank account" for strength, God's power was far beyond those numbers, and Persia, like the other empires, collapsed.

CHAPTER 4
BIBLE with HELLENISTIC EMPIRE

The books of the Bible related to Hellas

Amos, Isaiah, Jeremiah, Ezekiel, Daniel, the intermediate 400 year history between the Old Testament and the New etc.

History in the Old Testament and the New Testament

The last book of the Old Testament is written by the prophet Malachi. The first book of the New Testament is the Gospel of Matthew. You can turn the page from Malachi to Matthew in under a second; however, there is a span of four hundred years between the writing of the two books, four hundred years of silence from God.

In the time between the last verse of Malachi and the first verse of Matthew, the message of the two prophets turned from one of judgment to one of hope. Malachi ends with these words from God, "See, I will send the prophet Elijah to you before that great and dreadful day of the Lord comes. He will turn the hearts of the parents to their children, and the hearts of the children to their parents; or else I will come and strike the land with total destruction"(Malachi 4:5-6). And Matthew begins with an introduction of Jesus, who is the very hope for our salvation, "This is the genealogy of Jesus the Messiah the son of David, the son of Abraham" (Matthew 1:1).

There are many opinions on why God was silent, not even sending

Parthenon Temple of Acropolis

one prophet, during that time span.[44] Some argue that there were in fact prophets at that time, but that they just are not mentioned in the Bible. What we do know is that the prophets we read about in the Old Testament were all out of the picture by then.

Like the other prophets of the Old Testament, Malachi carried a message of judgment and forgiveness to the men and women of Judah who were practicing idolatry and were not committed to following God's ways. Through the prophet, God reminded them of His love and hastened them to get their act together and ready their hearts for Him.

But the people of Judah displayed a degree of arrogance and pride toward the Lord and questioned His love for them. "I have loved you," says the LORD. "But you ask, 'How have you loved us?'"(Malachi 1:2). It seems ludicrous that the people of Israel questioned God's love. After all, He had taken care of this one nation for sixteen hundred years, since the time of Abraham, and delivered them on many occasions out of the hands of their enemies. Though God had been faithful to Israel, He could not say the same about her.

In Malachi 1:7-9 God expresses His anger over how the people have defiled him by offering unclean sacrifices. God rhetorically questions whether they would make the same offerings to the Persian governor and expect to avoid punishment.

The ultimate expression of God's love for the people of Israel — and for us today — would come four hundred years later in the form of the Messiah who would later die for our sins to offer us the gift of eternal life (see John 3:16).

In the time of God's silence following the book of Malachi, King Alexander III of Macedonia, known as Alexander the Great, began expanding the Hellenistic Empire beyond Persia's borders into Southwest Asia, the Near East, and the Middle East. He sent his scholars and engineers to fuse Greek culture with the cultures of the newly conquered nations. This was how Hellenism originated.

The Rise of Macedonia and Daniel's Prediction of the Hellenistic Empire

I've talked about the incredible victories Greece claimed in battles such as Marathon, Salamis, and Mycale that eventually led to the demise of the Persian Empire. At that time, there was a growing competition brewing between the two Greek city-states of Sparta, which had a powerful army, and Athens, which had a powerful navy. This conflict resulted in the twenty-seven-year long Peloponnesian Wars that began in 431 BC. An Athens historian named Thucydides wrote about this event in *The History of the Peloponnesian War*. Sparta ultimately defeated Athens in these battles and became the leader of Greece. She would, however, continue to fight more wars to defend her status as a polis state until the end of her supremacy around 371 BC.

During the Peloponnesian Wars, a new force of politics was on the horizon. The Macedonians were a civilization with different customs, language, and way of life than the Greeks. Because of these notable differences, the Greeks referred to the Macedonians as barbarians.

King Philip II, the father of Alexander the Great, lived from 382 BC until 336 BC. As the leader of Macedonia, he expanded the country into a great and powerful force. He created an infantry of professional foot soldiers (civilians were used prior to this time) and equipped them with long spears. These soldiers, known as Foot Companions, made up the Macedonian Phalanx and were greatly feared. Alexander observed the techniques of his father's military experience and implemented what he learned into his own army when he took to the throne.

After King Philip II established a powerful army he gained strong political footing. In 356 BC, he discovered a gold mine in the town of Crenides, which helped him secure tremendous wealth. He changed the name of the city to Philippi, the same one mentioned in the New Testament. Philippi would become the location of the first church plant in Europe, formed during the Apostle Paul's second missionary journey as detailed in the book of Acts.

After a series of conquests, King Philip II conquered the entire country of Greece in 338 BC. That same year, the king created an organization called the League of Corinth, where all the states in Greece promised not to wage war against each other and to maintain peace. Not long after, King Philip II rallied the members together to battle the Persian Empire. However, he would not live to see the destruction of his enemy. In 336 BC, during the early part of the war against Persia, King Philip II was killed and his son, Alexander III, succeeded him on the throne.

Philip II of Macedon
(Cabinet des Médailles)

Two hundred and fifty years earlier, the prophet Daniel prophesied about the rise of King Alexander III and the Hellenistic Empire(see Daniel 7:6; 8:3-8, 21-22; 11:3). According to Josephus's *Antiquities of the Jews*, King Alexander III visited Jerusalem and made sacrifices to God. There he was shown the prophecies of Daniel and was surprised to discover he was the central figure of the prophetic revelation.

> "After that, I looked, and there before me was another beast, one that looked like a leopard. And on its back it had four wings like those of a bird. This beast had four heads, and it was given authority to rule"(Daniel 7:6).

> "The shaggy goat is the king of Greece, and the large horn between its eyes is the first king. The four horns that replaced the one that was broken off represent four kingdoms that will emerge from his nation but will not have the same power"(Daniel 8:21-22).

> "Then a mighty king will arise, who will rule with great power and do as he pleases"(Daniel 11:3) .

Alexander's Journey to the Throne and His Teacher, Aristotle

Olympias, Alexander's mother, was the fourth wife of King Philip II. Since all of his wives except for Olympias gave birth to daughters, Alexander's position as the king's heir was secure[45] and peace ruled in the palace. However, when Philip II married his seventh wife, Cleopatra, she became pregnant and drama ensued.

Atalos, Cleopatra's uncle, insisted that if she gave birth to a son, the

Alexander the Great _by Rembrandt

boy should become the rightful heir to the throne.[46] When nineteen-year-old Alexander heard this, he got angry and threw a wine glass at Atalos. King Philip II was angered by that and almost stabbed Alexander with his sword.[47] Alexander and his mother had no choice but to flee in exile to her hometown, Epirus. Fortunately, the drama was short-winded. Cleopatra gave birth to a girl, and Alexander returned home and maintained his position as next in line for the kingship.

When Alexander was still a young boy, King Philip II searched for a good teacher to educate his son. He found the perfect man for the job — Aristotle, the famous Greek philosopher who was a pillar of the entire Greek community. The result was that when Alexander came to rule the Hellenistic Empire, his leadership style encompassed more of a philosophical side as compared to the rulers of other empires.

Years prior to hiring Aristotle, King Philip II had destroyed the city of Stagira, the philosopher's hometown. In payment for the teacher's services to his son, King Philip II agreed to rebuild Stagira. He also gave to Aristotle the Temple of the Nymphs to use as his son's classroom.[48] You can visit that very place today.

Alexander learned from Aristotle not only about morality, politics, science, and literature but also profound doctrines unknown to the general public. Some time later, when King Alexander III was in Asia, he heard news that Aristotle had published those very private theories in a book. Alexander sent a letter complaining to his tutor. This letter and Aristotle's reply is found in *Plutarch's Lives*.

Bust of Aristotle
[National Museum of Rome]

"Alexander to Aristotle greeting. You have not done well to publish your books of oral doctrine; for what is there now that we excel others in, if those things which we have been particularly instructed in be laid open to all? For my part, I assure you, I had rather excel others in the knowledge of what is excellent, than in the extent of my power and dominion. Farewell." And Aristotle, soothing this passion for preeminence, speaks, in his excuse for himself, of these doctrines, as in fact both published and not published: as indeed, to say the truth, his books on metaphysics are written in a style which makes them useless for ordinary teaching, and instructive only, in the way of memoranda, for those who have been already conversant in that sort of learning.[49]

The Conquests of Alexander the Great

Not only was King Alexander III a learned man, he is known as one of the greatest military leaders of all time. Since he was a boy, he was anxious that his father had conquered too much land. Alexander worried that when he ascended the throne, there would be no more territory by which to expand the empire.[50] When Alexander became king after his father's death, he wanted to immediately set out on an expedition.

However, there was a fire he had to put out before he could focus on the conquest of land. When the Greek city-states of Athens, Thebes, Aetolia, and Sparta heard about King Philip II's death they rebelled against

Macedonia. King Alexander III set out to suppress these revolts and reconvene the League of Corinth, the peace accord organization his father created. When Sparta and Thebes rebelled a second time, however, Alexander mercilessly destroyed Thebes and used them as an example to teach the other Greek states a lesson.[51] The point was well taken.

The Battle of Alexander at Issus
by Albrecht Altdorfer

In 334 BC King Alexander III was ready to conquer Persia and invaded Asia Minor. The king took with him about forty thousand soldiers[52] who were paid a salary out of the Macedonian royal treasury. Some of the soldiers were worried that the king would go broke. His faithful and loyal servants believed in and respected him so much they returned their paychecks to the king so he would have enough finances to fund the war.[53]

King Alexander III and his army won a great victory in 333 BC at the Battle of Issus, which gave him control of most of Asia. He continued on to Egypt the following year and conquered that country as well.

Perhaps the king's greatest military accomplishment was his conquest of Tyre in 332 BC. The Old Testament book of Ezekiel includes prophetic messages about the demise of the Persian city.

> "They will destroy the walls of Tyre and pull down her towers; I will scrape away her rubble and make her a bare rock"(Ezekiel 26:4).

> "Son of man, take up a lament concerning Tyre. Say to Tyre, situated at the gateway to the sea, merchant of peoples on many

> coasts, 'This is what the Sovereign LORD says: "'You say, Tyre, "I am perfect in beauty." Your domain was on the high seas; your builders brought your beauty to perfection. They made all your timbers of juniper from Senir; they took a cedar from Lebanon to make a mast for you. Of oaks from Bashan they made your oars; of cypress wood from the coasts of Cyprus they made your deck, adorned with ivory. Fine embroidered linen from Egypt was your sail and served as your banner; your awnings were of blue and purple from the coasts of Elishah. Men of Sidon and Arvad were your oarsmen; your skilled men, Tyre, were aboard as your sailors"(Ezekiel 27:2-8).

> "Son of man, say to the ruler of Tyre, 'This is what the Sovereign Lord says: "'In the pride of your heart you say, "I am a god; I sit on the throne of a god in the heart of the seas." But you are a mere mortal and not a god, though you think you are as wise as a god" (Ezekiel 28:2).

Tyre was a wealthy port city that controlled the Mediterranean Sea. She had a flourishing trade with various countries of the Middle East, and reaped the rewards of profitable businesses like making and selling purple dye and building ships. Her citizens enjoyed prosperity and wealth at a level unimaginable even to us today. Sitting in the lap of luxury, they had no fear of anything, especially not God.

When Kings David and Solomon ruled the nation of Israel, she was on friendly terms with people of Tyre. As the years went by, however, the courtesies evaporated, and Tyre started selling the captives of Israel to the nation of Edom. This betrayal did not go unnoticed by God. He used prophets like Ezekiel to relay the message that Tyre would be punished for her mistreatment of His people.

In eighth century BC, immediately before the northern Kingdom of Israel was destroyed, the prophet Amos prophesied about Tyre. "For three sins of Tyre, even for four, I will not relent. Because she sold whole communities of captives to Edom, disregarding a treaty of brotherhood, I will send fire on the walls of Tyre that will consume her fortresses"(Amos 1:9-10).

The prophet Isaiah also spoke of God's warning against Tyre. He prophesied that the arrogance and pride of the people for having accumulated wealth and prosperity would eventually turn into sorrow and weeping. "A prophecy against Tyre: Wail, you ships of Tarshish! For Tyre is destroyed and left without house or harbor. From the land of Cyprus word has come to them. Be silent, you people of the island and you merchants of Sidon, whom the seafarers have enriched. On the great waters came the grain of the Shihor; the harvest of the Nile was the revenue of Tyre, and she became the marketplace of the nations"(Isaiah 23:1-3).

God offered these prophecies to make known His all-consuming power, but I'm sure the captives found them hard to believe. They saw Tyre as a financially dominant, strong, and invincible power. God, however, needed to remind them that He is more powerful than the most powerful of nations. True to God's Word, King Alexander III ultimately destroyed the city by using a creative and impressive strategy.

King Alexander III wanted to conquer Tyre in order to secure the supply route from Macedonia. Since Tyre was on an island with walls all the way up to the sea, she proved to be a challenging conquest. The citizens of Tyre felt confident they would not be invaded because of their unique geographical location along with the additional manpower they acquired through their ally, Carthage, a North African colony. For seven months, King Alexander III attempted to invade Tyre without any success. Finally, he had an idea.

Because the king could not attack Tyre from the sea, he built a causeway to lead into the city. King Alexander III mobilized two hundred ships and ten thousand soldiers and had huge rocks rolled in from mountains to build this road.[54] When the causeway was finished, Alexander's army used the bridge to launch an intensive attack along a south wall (and weak point) of the city, and with help from conquered Persian navies and one hundred and twenty ships from Cyprus, managed to occupy the city. Most of the people of Tyre were either killed or sold into slavery. God's prophecies spoken through Isaiah, Ezekiel, and Amos were fulfilled.

Tyre remained subject to the Hellenistic Empire until it was destroyed by the Roman Empire around 30 BC. The city was granted historical significance when archeological remains were discovered in that area, leading UNESCO (United Nations Educational Scientific, and Cultural Organization) to declare Tyre a world heritage site in 1984.

After years of being under Persian rule, Judea (a Greek and Roman adaptation of the word "Judah") found itself under the rule of King Alexander III around 332 BC. When the king's army arrived in Judea, they were welcomed with open arms. The high priest wore purple and red clothes and a hat with the name of God inscribed on it and a gold plaque attached to it, as a sign of respect to the king. King Alexander III reciprocated similar respects.

Alexander the Great in the Temple of Jerusalem_by Sebastiano Conca

According to Flavius Josephus,[55] the king had a dream before he set out on his expedition to conquer land. In that dream, as he was strategizing about invading Asia, a man dressed as a Jewish high priest appeared and told him that he would guide his army and help him to occupy Persia. When he saw the high priest in Jerusalem, King Alexander III was reminded of that dream. During his reign, he treated the Jewish people well and with fairness. He did not even require them to pay tribute in the sabbatical year.

Alexander's Death and the Division of Hellenistic Empire

Paul Johnson wrote that King Alexander III "cracked the Persian empire like a rotten egg".[56] Many of the places he conquered welcomed his forces as a liberating army instead of resisting the occupation. This is why he and his men did not pillage many cities, save a few like Persepolis.

The Greek historian Diodorus Siculus wrote in *Library of History* that King Alexander III thought of Persepolis as "the most hateful city in Persia." After he captured her in 330 BC, he ordered his soldiers to pillage the city and her inhabitants. The destruction and brutalities carried out by the king's men were beyond description.

While King Alexander III was busy capturing the cities of Susa, Babylon, and Persepolis, King Darius III had fled to Ecbatana and tried to restore his military might. He didn't last long. The Persian king was betrayed and murdered in 330 BC at the hand of his cousin and was no longer a threat to King Alexander III. From that time on, the region was put under the hegemony of the Hellenistic Empire.

After King Alexander III occupied the whole of Persia, he continued

The Septuagint, LXX

his expedition to the east. He could not, however, expand the empire further than the Indus River basin because his soldiers grew tired of the long war and refused to continue to serve. On his way back from his last expedition, King Alexander III died of an unknown disease in 323 BC. He was thirty-two years old. Some say he died of malaria; others suggest he died of a fever that developed after he took a cold bath.

His sudden death brought about a great change in the Hellenistic Empire. It was divided and eventually came to be ruled by four of the king's generals. Among the four, three established their own dynasties and one established a small kingdom called Attalid based at Pergamum in north Asia Minor. Pergamum later became a center of arts and literature.[57)] The other three dynasties include the Antigonid in Macedon and central Greece; the Ptolemaic in Egypt; and the Seleucid in Syria and Mesopotamia. None of leaders of these dynasties were powerful enough to unify the empire as the sole monarch.[58)]

The Battle for Jerusalem

In 301 BC, Ptolemy I ruled Judea, but did not impose the Hellenistic religious laws onto the small kingdom and allowed Judea to keep her religious traditions.[59)] When the next king, Ptolemy II Philadelphus, ascended to the throne, he also permitted the Jews to worship God. He even selected seventy interpreters to translate the Hebrew Old Testament of the Bible into Greek. This document was known as the Septuagint. This translation allowed the Jewish Diaspora living in Greek cities to read the Bible in that language.

According to a legend of Judaism, after the seventy men finished their translations, which were done separately, the documents were compared. Not a single word of difference was found among them.[60] We can conclude that the translation was directed by God and led by the Holy Spirit.

For the most part, the kings of the Ptolemy dynasty enacted an accommodating and lenient policy concerning religion and the customs of the people over which they ruled. However, because of the ongoing battle between the Ptolemy and Seleucid dynasties, the people of Judea went through many hardships, particularly after Judea was handed over to the Seleucid dynasty.

In 198 BC, the Seleucid King Antiochus III took the land of Judea away from Ptolemy and amalgamated it with his dynasty. As the new ruler of Judea, Antiochus III respected the Jews and was a fair leader. That favor ended when his son, Antiochus IV, took the throne in 175 BC.

Let's go back in time so you can see the genesis of the conflict that erupted in Judea. Rome was becoming a powerful force in the Mediterranean because of her victories in the first Punic War (264-241 BC) and the second Punic War (218-202 BC). After the second Punic war, Greece, which was ruled by King Philip V of Macedonia, appealed to Rome to help her gain independence. Rome waged war against Macedonia and in 197 BC, with a decisive win in the Battle of Cynoscephalae, freed the Greeks from Macedonian control.

The Aetolians, who were living in central Greece, were not satisfied with mere independence from the Macedonians. They also wanted to drive the Romans, who were a visible presence in their country, completely out of their territory. The Aetolians asked the Seleucid dynasty, ruled by King

Antiochus III, to intervene. Antiochus reigned over the largest expanse of land in the Hellenistic Empire and was known as the most powerful monarch.

King Antiochus III gladly accepted the request of the Aetolians. In 192 BC, he invaded Greece with a puny force. Rome, with Philip V as a surprising ally, defeated Antiochus in the 191 BC Battle of Thermopylae. King Antiochus III ended up fleeing Greece with a small number of surviving soldiers. Upon returning home, the king replenished his military with the intention of using Hannibal of Carthage in the next round of war. Hannibal, one of the world's greatest military commanders, had been living in Seleucid territory after he fled from Rome. When Rome's leaders heard the news, they pulled out their secret "weapon," Scipio Africanus, a famed general who had defeated Hannibal in the second Punic War.

The Battle of Magnesia broke out in 190 BC and resulted in a great victory for Rome. The Seleucid dynasty was significantly crippled, as the defeat required them to relinquish control of Asia Minor and the Aegean Sea to Rome. A tremendous war penalty of fifteen thousand talents, five thousand of which was due immediately, was imposed on King Antiochus III. In order to come up with the money, the king plundered a temple. The people of his kingdom were outraged and soon after, he was assassinated.[61]

The next king, Seleucus IV, was also pressured by Rome to pay a hefty tribute. He was murdered after reigning for twelve years, and his younger brother, Antiochus IV, took the throne and ruled from 175 to 163 BC. King Antiochus IV called himself Epiphanes, meaning "incarnation of God," but the Jews called him Epimanes, meaning "mad man."

King Antiochus IV imposed unprecedented suffering upon the Jewish people from the moment he stepped in as ruler. The king forced the people of his territory to accept and embrace the Hellenistic customs and culture. The Jewish people, however, strongly rejected Hellenistic ideologies.

The king tried to convert the Jewish religious community by replacing their high priest with his brother, Jason, who had a more favorable view of Greek culture. King Antiochus IV also put Jason in charge of the public treasury, the monies accumulated through taxes and the temple offerings. The new high priest planned to make Jewish culture more Hellenistic and even intended to change the name of Jerusalem to Antioch.

A man named Menelaus ousted Jason in 172 BC. The overthrow was supported by the king for two reasons: Menelaus offered to pay King Antiochus IV more tribute than Jason, and he proposed a more ambitious policy to Hellenize the people of Judea. Menelaus came from a family of priests and had the backing of the Jewish conservatives, but he overestimated the support of the people of Judea. Many refused to adhere to his strict policies, especially the one that prohibited them from making sacrifices to God in the temple and, instead, forced them to worship Zeus. The Jews who refused to worship the Greek god were put to death. (It is common belief among historians that these Jews were the first-ever martyrs.) Angered at the attempt to purge the Jewish religion, the people revolted against King Antiochus IV and Menelaus.

In 170 BC, King Antiochus IV made his move to conquer Egypt, which was ruled by King Ptolemy VI. But Rome had other ideas. The ever powerful and growing Roman Empire threatened Antiochus IV with war if he didn't leave Egypt alone. Defeated and licking his wounds, the king returned to Jerusalem. He irrationally believed that his defeat in Egypt had to do with the people of Judea not accepting the Hellenistic customs.

King Antiochus IV flew into a violent rage and destroyed the Judean city. He desecrated the temple by making a sacrifice of a dead pig to the Greek god Zeus, the highest abomination in the eyes of the Jews.[62] He massacred the residents of Jerusalem. He killed circumcised children and hung their dead bodies around their mothers' necks. The king bound six hundred priests with rope and ruthlessly killed them by running chariots over their bodies.

The Hasmonean Dynasty and the Dissolution of the Hellenistic Empire

There were particular groups of Jews who were exceptionally vocal in their opposition to King Antioch IV. Mattathias the Hasmonean, who came from an ancient lineage of Jewish priests, challenged King Antiochus IV's order to worship Greek gods. He even went so far as to kill a government official who tried to force him to take part in idolatry. Following the murder, Mattathias went into hiding with his sons, who also rebelled against the Seleucid dynasty.

Mattathias' sons Judah, Jonathan, and Simon fought to allow the Jews to freely worship God and maintain their cultural customs and religious traditions. Judah, given the surname Maccabee, led the Maccabee Revolution beginning in 167 BC in order to drive the Greeks out of Jerusalem. Through a string of battles and subsequent victories, Judah proceeded to defeat the Seleucid forces and, in 164 BC, purified the temple of Jerusalem and reinstated Jewish practices. Antiochus blamed Menelaus for this Jewish revolution and had him killed.

In 161 BC, the Hasmoneans broke all ties with the Seleucid dynasty and became allies with Rome. The Seleucids finally gave up their attempts to Hellenize Judea and in 152 BC appointed Judah's brother, Jonathan, as the high priest of Judea. In 142 BC, with Jonathan's brother Simon now officiating as high priest, Judea finally gained her official independence. This marked the beginning of the Hasmonean dynasty, founded by the Maccabee brothers.

After Simon, Judea was ruled by John Hyrcanus (134-104 BC); his eldest son Aristobulus (104-103 BC); his younger brother Alexander Jannaeus (103-76 BC), who married Aristobulus's widow, Alexandra Salome; and

Alexandra Salome (76-67 BC). In the last days of the Hasmonean dynasty, Hyrcanus II (67 BC) and Aristobulus II (67-63 BC), both sons of Alexandra Salome, competed against each other for the throne, only to lose control of Judea to Rome in 63 BC.

I'd like to take a look into the life of John Hyrcanus. He was inspired to restore the Davidic kingdom. He studied the books of Joshua and Samuel to learn the will of God. He believed God wanted the Jews to inherit the entire land of Palestine; he felt it was his duty to conquer it and root out any foreign cults or religious sects. His efforts included destroying Samaria and burning down the Greek-style city of Scythopolis. He also killed those who would not convert to the Jewish faith.

When his son Alexander Jannaeus became king in 103 BC, he expanded on his father's vision, conquering more land and forcing people to convert to Judaism or choose death. The Hasmonean dynasty eventually became corrupt, and the competition between Hyrcanus II and Aristobulus II caused Judea to suffer a costly civil war that, according to Flavius Josephus, lasted six years and took the lives of fifty thousand Jews.

In 63 BC, Antipater, a native of Edom and father of Herod the Great, became a powerful official under the Hasmonean dynasty. Antipater was from a family who was forced to convert to Judaism under the rule of John Hyrcanus.[63] While serving under Hyrcanus II, Antipater thought it would be better for Judea to become subject to Rome than to have civil war. Rome took control of Jerusalem and all the territories conquered by the Hasmoneans. Hyrancus II was appointed high priest, and Antipater the governor, of Judea.

God's Management of the Universe

The keyword I connected with the Hellenistic Empire is "amalgamate." King Alexander III combined Greek philosophy and culture with that of the East and created a new culture, Hellenism. Similar to the Assyrians, who eliminated boundaries of nations by mixing races, Hellenism formed a Cosmopolitan blend of cultures. While the philosophies of the Hellenistic Empire weren't necessarily wrong, they still did not require people to conform to the ways of God. The prosperity of a nation is not possible through mere human tactics, but through God alone. Proverbs 19:21 tells us, "Many are the plans in a man's heart, but it is the LORD's purpose that prevails."

I've said many times that God created all things and set the boundary of residence for each individual and each nation. I believe God intended for each country to be a separate entity with its own cultures, traditions, and customs. It's our responsibility to respect each other's individuality and uniqueness, just as the Apostle Paul, who was a Jew born in Rome, did during his ministry.

He wrote, "Though I am free and belong to no one, I have made myself a slave to everyone, to win as many as possible. To the Jews I became like a Jew, to win the Jews. To those under the law I became like one under the law (though I myself am not under the law), so as to win those under the law. To those not having the law I became like one not having the law (though I am not free from God's law but am under Christ's law), so as to win those not having the law. To the weak I became weak, to win the weak. I have become all things to all people so that by all possible means I might save some. I do all this for the sake of the gospel, that I may share in its blessings. I have become all things to all people so that by all possible means I might save some" (1 Corinthians 9:19-23).

Paul was not saying that he compromised or changed his beliefs, culture, or customs to manipulate people to come to Christ. He simply adapted his teaching to his particular audience so they could understand and be touched by the message of salvation. Both human beings and nations are different from one another. It is God's desire that we respect those differences and work together for good of the Lord.

The Rise and Fall of the 5 Empires in the Bible

CHAPTER 5
BIBLE with ROMAN EMPIRE

The books of the Bible related to Rome

All the 27 books from Matthew to Revelation

The entire New Testament is connected to the Roman Empire — from Jesus' birth in Bethlehem; Matthew's occupation as a tax collector; the Son of God's crucifixion; the Apostle John's exile to Patmos; to the Apostle Paul's' missionary journey. Much information is available in both the Bible and world history to learn about this empire.

The Beginning of the Roman Empire

There are many classic quotes about Rome. "Rome was not built in a day" is one of them. This is indeed true in a literal and figurative sense. How can a country be established in one day? Another saying is, "All roads lead to Rome." While today it means that there are many ways to get to the same destination, the quote originated from the impressive engineering of the city's roadways.

The founding of Rome is surrounded by myth. One particular story stems from twin brothers, Romulus and Remus, who were born in the eighth century BC. This legend tells us that the twin boys were born to a vestal virgin and abandoned. The babies were raised by a she-wolf who breastfed them. Later, a shepherd adopted and cared for the twins. The boys grew up to be excellent warriors, and one day decided to found their own city. After Romulus received an omen from the gods about building the city, he murdered Remus. Thus, Rome was born.

When Rome fought against Carthage in the three Punic Wars, which lasted one hundred and twenty years, she quickly expanded into a powerful country. As Rome conquered more land over the years, she grew so big the Mediterranean Sea seemed like a mere lake.

Rome was governed as a republic until Julius Caesar came to power. He was appointed *dictator perpetuus* by the Senate in 44 BC. As a popular politician and successful general, Caesar wished to abandon the republic rule and establish a new blueprint for Rome. He felt strongly that the country should adopt the imperial system. Other powerful leaders in the Senate did not support Caesar's views. A month after his appointment, he was assassinated in one of the most famous conspiracy plots, spearheaded by his friend Marcus Brutus.

Ironically, after Caesar's death it became clear that such a large empire could not be ruled in the ways of the ancient republic. In 27 BC, after a long period of civil war, the Senate appointed Caesar's heir, his adopted grandnephew Julius Caesar Octavius, as the first emperor.

Octavius's given name was Gaius Octavius. After Julius Caesar's death, he took the name Gaius Julius Caesar Octavianus for a while. When the Senate gave him

This gold coin reveals the veiled head of Julius Caesar on the front side with emblem CAESAR COS TER". At the back of the coin is a lituus, a jug and an axe with emblem "A. HIRTIVS P. R".

power to rule all the affairs of the Roman Empire as the first emperor they named him Augustus (meaning "exalted one").

Augustus, who ruled during the time of Jesus' birth, is known for establishing Pax Romana, meaning "Roman peace," which lasted from 27 BC to 180 AD. Similar terms have been used to describe periods of civil order in other countries, including Pax Britannica and Pax Americana. The Roman citizens enjoyed a period of time without war, but it was not necessarily a time of peace for the vassal states of Rome. Judea in particular was constantly plagued with civil conflict.

Julius Caesar was the first known leader to manufacture currency with his picture on it. Today, of course, this is common practice. This brings to mind an interesting story about Jesus found in the Gospel of Matthew. With an ulterior motive, the Pharisees asked Jesus a question about paying taxes to the Roman government. One of Caesar's coins was used to make a point.

> "Then the Pharisees went out and laid plans to trap him in his words. They sent their disciples to him along with the Herodians. "Teacher," they said, "we know that you are a man of integrity and that you teach the way of God in accordance with the truth. You

aren't swayed by others, because you pay no attention to who they are. Tell us then, what is your opinion? Is it right to pay the imperial tax to Caesar or not?"
But Jesus, knowing their evil intent, said, "You hypocrites, why are you trying to trap me? Show me the coin used for paying the tax." They brought him a denarius, and he asked them, "Whose image is this? And whose inscription?"
"Caesar's," they replied.
Then he said to them, "So give back to Caesar what is Caesar's, and to God what is God's."
When they heard this, they were amazed. So they left him and went away"(Matthew 22:15-22).

Herod the Great

At the end of the previous chapter, we learned how Judea came to be ruled by the Roman Empire. Following that battle, Antipater, the father of Herod the Great, went to work for the Roman General Pompey. But the partnership was short-lived. When Julius Caesar Augustus (then Octavius) and Pompey went to war against each other, Antipater shifted his support to Caesar, who in turn granted him Roman citizenship and appointed him procurator of Judea.

During his rule, Antipater put his son Herod in charge of governing

A Model of Herod's Temple
in the Israel Museum in Jerusalem

Galilee under the Jewish puppet king Hyrcanus II. In 40 BC, Herod's rival, Antigonus, invaded Jerusalem and unseated Hyrcanus. Herod fled to Rome and begged the government to intervene. In 37 BC the Roman Senate appointed him the king of Judea. To solidify his position as king, Herod married Mariamme, a Hasmonean princess who was considered befitting of the throne. Herod was king from 37 BC until 4 AD. He was called Herod the Great and was known to be a brilliant, capable, ruthless, and brutal leader.

Famous for his construction projects, Herod the Great built many new cities, including Caesarea Maritima, which was dedicated to Emperor Augustus. Caesarea became a major political and military center, and Herod had a great bronze statue of himself erected there. The city is mentioned many times in the Bible. For instance, Acts 10 tells us of a centurion named Cornelius who was from Caesarea and who met with the Apostle Peter.

Around 19 BC, Herod the Great started renovating and expanding the temple in Jerusalem. It took forty-six years to complete the construction. Herod's Temple was world famous. There is even a record that the Gentiles made sacrifices there to win the favor of the Jews. Marcus Agrippa, for instance, who was Emperor Augustus's right-hand man, sacrificed a hundred bulls in the temple in 15 BC.

Quoting Flavius Josephus's description of the temple, Paul Johnson wrote in his book *History of the Jews* how huge embankments were created around the temple and filled with broken stones to increase the size of the temple mound. This created quite a majestic look. Also, Herod built two large bridges to connect the temple with the city. The structure was bigger than Solomon's temple. While Herod the Great didn't spend a lot of money to decorate the inside of the temple, he lavished the exterior with ornate embellishments, coating it with silver and gold. The temple quickly garnered attention from all over the world and became a magnificent tourist attraction.

The Herodian Dynasty

The lineage of the house of Herod, many of whom are mentioned in the New Testament, is rather extensive. It's important to make the distinction between the different leaders so you can understand which Herod is related to which historical and Biblical event. While Herod the Great had nine sons through multiple marriages, I will only focus on the ones who reigned over the territory of ancient Israel.

The Herodian dynasty, which began around 37 BC, walked the tightrope between the last days of the Hasmonean dynasty and the beginning of the Roman Empire. Many people find it surprising that the Herods had Jewish roots, as they were descendants from the land of Edom.

Herod the Great ruled as king of Judea when Jesus was born, and he died shortly after. Many of us are familiar with the story of the birth of Christ. Herod had heard rumors from the wise men that a child was born who would one day be king. He was terrified by what he considered to be a threat to his throne. "After Jesus was born in Bethlehem in Judea, during the time of King Herod, Magi from the east came to Jerusalem and asked, "Where is the one who has been born king of the Jews? We saw his star when it rose and have come to worship him." When King Herod heard this he was disturbed, and all Jerusalem with him"(Matthew 2:1-3).

Though he desired to visit the newborn, intending to kill him, Herod the Great didn't know where Jesus was. So the king issued a decree that would indirectly eliminate this potential threat. He ordered the murder of all baby boys under the age of two. Joseph and Mary were warned about this through a vision from the Lord, and they fled to Egypt. They returned to Judea after Herod the Great had died and his son, Herod Archelaus, had ascended the throne.

> "After Herod died, an angel of the Lord appeared in a dream to Joseph in Egypt and said, "Get up, take the child and his mother and go to the land of Israel, for those who were trying to take the child's life are dead." So he got up, took the child and his mother and went to the land of Israel. But when he heard that Archelaus was reigning in Judea in place of his father Herod, he was afraid to go there. Having been warned in a dream, he withdrew to the district of Galilee, and he went and lived in a town called Nazareth. So was fulfilled what was said through the prophets, that he would be called a Nazarene"(Matthew 2:19-23).

Upon Herod the Great's death in 4 AD, his kingdom was divided among his sons who ruled as tetrarchs over specific territories. Herod Archelaus, mentioned in the above passage of Scripture, was given the regions of Judea, Samaria, and Edom. Herod Antipas ruled over Galilee and Perarea. Herod Philip II was the tetrarch of the Golan Heights.

Because of the oppressive and violent rule of Herod Archelaus Joseph and Mary settled in Galilee instead of Judea. They weren't the only ones who despised the policies and politics of the king. The nobles of Judea and Samaria opposed Archelaus and even dispatched a delegate to petition the Roman emperor to remove the king from power. In 6 AD, Herod Archelaus was dethroned, and Judea became a Roman province ruled by a prefect.

Herod Antipas makes an appearance in the Bible during Jesus' three-year public ministry. In Matthew 13:32, Jesus calls him a fox. I find it interesting that our Lord referred to this leader as a cunning and shrewd animal. When Herod Antipas heard about Jesus and the miracles he was performing, he was convinced it was John the Baptist(see Matthew 14:2). When Jesus was arrested prior to the crucifixion, Herod Antipas was the one who questioned Jesus.

John the Baptist also had encounters with this king as told in the Gospel of Matthew. While Herod Antipas was married to Nabatea, the daughter of the king of Arabia, he wanted to take another woman as his wife. He divorced his first wife and married Herodias, his brother's ex-wife. John the Baptist expressed his disdain to Herod, saying, "It is not lawful for you to have her"(Matthew 14:3-4). As a result of his public rebuke of the king's immorality, John the Baptist was thrown in prison. Herod Antipas ultimately ordered the death of John the Baptist and had the follower of Christ beheaded.

Herod Philip II, the half brother of Herod Antipas and Herod Archelaus, is briefly mentioned in Luke 3:1. He was the meekest of Herod the Great's sons and was respected by the people. Jesus was able to minister in the area that Herod Philip II ruled without any problems. Herod Philip II rebuilt the city of Caesarea Philippi (not to be confused with Caesarea Maritima, the city built by his father) and made it the administrative capital. The Bible mentions this city in Matthew 16:13, "When Jesus came to the region of Caesarea Philippi, he asked his disciples, "Who do people say the Son of Man is?"

The Preaching of St. John the Baptist
by Baciccio

Herod Agrippa I was the

grandson of Herod the Great and the brother of Herodias. His father, Aristobulus IV, was executed by his own father in 7 BC. Herod Agrippa I was then sent to Rome to live in the palace. There he befriended two young men, Caligula and Claudius, who would later become Roman emperors. Capitalizing on his friendship with Caligula, Herod Agrippa I gained the territories of his uncles Herod Antipas and Herod Philip II. By 41 AD, Herod Agrippa I had joined together and was reigning over all the territories that were once ruled by his grandfather, Herod the Great.

Herod Agrippa I is the king who appears in the book of Acts. In Acts 12 we read about his persecution of Christians, including the execution of James and the imprisonment of Peter. The same chapter also records his death. "On the appointed day Herod, wearing his royal robes, sat on his throne and delivered a public address to the people. They shouted, "This is the voice of a god, not of a man." Immediately, because Herod did not give praise to God, an angel of the Lord struck him down, and he was eaten by worms and died"(Acts 12:21-23).

When Herod Agrippa I died, his seventeen-year-old son Herod Agrippa II ascended the throne and became the last king of the Herodian dynasty. Because he was too young to rule, a Roman procurator named Cuspius Fadus was sent to rule most of Judea.

Tiberius, the Second Roman Emperor

After the death of Augustus in 14 AD, Tiberius Caesar Augustus took the throne and ruled from 14 to 37. The Bible mentions his reign during the time of Jesus' public ministry and crucifixion and the beginning of John the Baptist's public ministry. The book of Luke opens with the political map of Rome and Judea during his reign. "During the fifteenth year of Tiberius's reign, Pontius Pilate was the governor of Judea; Herod Antipas was the tetrarch of Galilee; Philip was the tetrarch of Iturea and Traconitis; and Lysanias ruled as the tetrarch of Abilene"(Luke 3:1).

Tiberius was Augustus's stepson but was not the emperor's first choice to inherit the throne. The succession only occurred because he didn't have an alternative. When Augustus was twenty-three years old, he divorced his first wife soon after the birth of their daughter, Julia. He fell madly in love with and married Livia, a woman who was already married and pregnant. She also had a three-year-old son, the future-emperor Tiberius, who lived with his biological father. After her new baby Drusus was born, Livia sent him to live with his father as well. She was eventually reunited with her sons after their biological father died, and the two boys came to live with her and their stepfather, Augustus.

Augustus and Livia tried desperately to produce an heir, but they did not bear any children together, which greatly upset the emperor. It was ironic that although he himself was adopted, he placed great value on blood relations. He even went so far as to force his only daughter Julia to marry Agrippa, his political ally and friend who was as old as he, to pass on the lineage. Julia gave birth to two sons; however, they died before Augustus needed to implement his plan of succession.

A Marble Head of the Empress Livia, Octavianus' Wife _ The British Museum

By that time, Tiberius was making a name for himself politically and militarily. Augustus still was not convinced

A Marble Head of the Emperor Tiberius
The British Museum

that his stepson should be the next emperor, but he quickly realized he had no choice. Tiberius would ascend to the throne under one condition — he would have to divorce his wife and marry Julia, who had been widowed by Agrippa. Although Tiberius loved his wife very much, he had to accept the request of his stepfather. During her marriage to Tiberius, Julia was found to have committed adultery, and her father sentenced her to exile. Tiberius remained a single man until his death.

About twelve years after Tiberius became emperor, he retreated to an island called Capri and lived a reclusive life. Many believe he wanted to avoid particular senators who did not share his political views. He carried out his royal duties from that island until his death.

The Governing of Judea and Various Religious Groups

In 26 AD, Tiberius appointed Pontius Pilate as governor of Judea. He ruled the land for ten years. Even though Judea was ruled as a Roman province, it was a self-controlled territory when it came to civil matters. The Roman governor's responsibilities included collecting taxes, maintaining order, and carrying out military details.

The rulers of Judea, namely the Sanhedrin, the judicial council of the Jewish people, controlled the day-to-day administration of the land. The Sanhedrin even had its own police force, which made it possible for them to arrest Jesus. When the Hasmonean dynasty came to an end, the Sanhedrin was recognized as the supreme ruling body of Judea and was involved in every aspect of Jewish life. When Jesus was preaching the Sermon on the Mount, he mentioned the Sanhedrin(see Matthew 5:22). The Gospels record how this same ruling body tried to trap and kill Jesus(see Matthew 26:59). They ultimately had Jesus arrested, condemned, and sentenced to die.

There were several different factions of political and religious influence among the Jewish leaders — the Sadducees (which made up most of the Sanhedrin), the Pharisees, and the Essenes. These political and religious parties instigated frequent spats and conflict among each other and the Jewish population in general.

The Sadducees, the most powerful religious leaders, were comprised of rich families and leading families of priests. They maintained religious power by being somewhat accepting of Roman culture. The Sadducees were fully in charge of managing the temple. In order to maintain the life of a religious noble, they pretended to keep the Law yet made moral compromises with their political power.

The Pharisees were a conservative and legalistic group of people. Joachim Jeremias wrote in his book that there were more than six thousand Pharisees in first century AD.[64)] The Pharisees believed in adhering to the oral law, the traditional manner in which ancient Israel verbally passed down laws. They were often at odds with the Sadducees, the more liberal religious group.

Though not talked about in the Bible, the Essenes were a religious sect mentioned in the Dead Sea Scrolls. They took a more mystical approach to religion and lived a secluded life. The Essenes were known for their asceticism, voluntary poverty, and abstinence from worldly pleasures.

While it seems that most of the religious leaders of Judea hated Jesus, there was one man named Joseph who respected the Messiah. He even

The Sanhedrin Council

asked Pontius Pilate for Jesus' body after his crucifixion so he could give the Messiah a proper burial.

"Joseph of Arimathea, a prominent member of the Council, who was himself waiting for the kingdom of God, went boldly to Pilate and asked for Jesus' body. Pilate was surprised to hear that he was already dead. Summoning the centurion, he asked him if Jesus had already died. When he learned from the centurion that it was so, he gave the body to Joseph. So Joseph bought some linen cloth, took down the body, wrapped it in the linen, and placed it in a tomb cut out of rock. Then he rolled a stone against the entrance of the tomb. Mary Magdalene and Mary the mother of Joseph saw where he was laid"(Mark 15:43-47).

Pontius Pilate and The Crucifixion of Jesus

Pontius Pilate was both a skillful politician and an excellent administrator, yet he faced much difficulty in ruling Judea. The Jewish religious leaders were very powerful and hard to manage and control. They also seemed to instigate conflict everywhere they went, whether among themselves or against the Roman government.

Perhaps the Jewish leaders' most vocal complaint to the Romans was about Jesus. They accused him of blasphemy, and their hatred of the Messiah sent the people of Judea into an uproar, ultimately paving the way to our Lord's death.

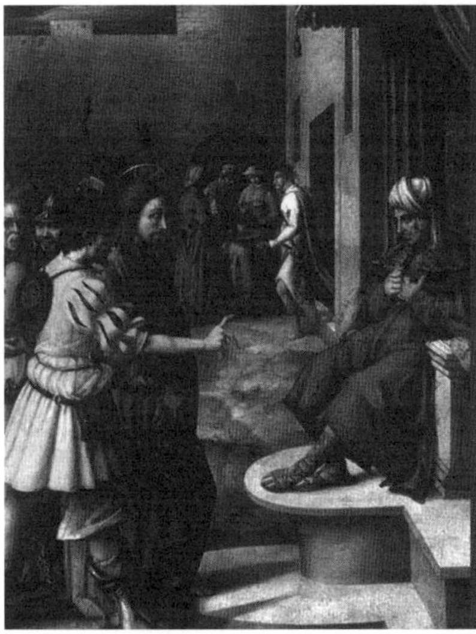
Jesus Christ before the high priest
by Francesco Bacchiacca

The most important event in the Bible that has ties to the Roman Empire is the crucifixion of Jesus. This event on which the foundation of Christianity was built took place during the time of Passover. Under the leadership of the high priest Caiaphas, the religious leaders of Judea plotted to kill Jesus. They bribed Judas, one of Jesus' disciples, to give them information about the Son of Man's whereabouts. The priests found Jesus in the Garden of Gethsemane and arrested him there. He was then brought before the Sanhedrin where he was questioned.

> "The chief priests and the whole Sanhedrin were looking for false evidence against Jesus so that they could put him to death. But they did not find any, though many false witnesses came forward. Finally two came forward and declared, "This fellow said, 'I am able to destroy the temple of God and rebuild it in three days.'"
> Then the high priest stood up and said to Jesus, "Are you not going to answer? What is this testimony that these men are bringing against you?" But Jesus remained silent.
> The high priest said to him, "I charge you under oath by the living God: Tell us if you are the Messiah, the Son of God."
> "You have said so," Jesus replied. "But I say to all of you: From now on you will see the Son of Man sitting at the right hand of the Mighty One and coming on the clouds of heaven."

Then the high priest tore his clothes and said, "He has spoken blasphemy! Why do we need any more witnesses? Look, now you have heard the blasphemy. What do you think?"
"He is worthy of death," they answered.
Then they spit in his face and struck him with their fists. Others slapped him and said, "Prophesy to us, Messiah. Who hit you?" (Matthew 26:59-68)

The next day, the people began to make plans for his execution and led Him to Pontius Pilate(see Matthew 27:1-2). Pilate questioned Jesus.

"Are you the king of the Jews?"
"You have said so," Jesus replied. When he was accused by the chief priests and the elders, he gave no answer.
Then Pilate asked him, "Don't you hear the testimony they are bringing against you?"
But Jesus made no reply, not even to a single charge — to the great amazement of the governor(Matthew 27:11-14).

What is Truth? Jesus and Pilate
by Nikolai Ge

Pilate did not believe him to be guilty and wanted to pardon Jesus. Instead he left the vote up to the people — they would decide if Jesus should be released or, alternatively, another prisoner named Barabbas. Matthew 27:15-17 tells us how it was custom during the time of Passover for the governor to release a prisoner. The Passover holiday was an occasion where Jews from all over would gather together. During these times, riots would frequently break out among the Jewish people who wanted to be independent of Roman rule. According to Flavius Josephus, one way the Romans tried to maintain peace was to allow the people to choose a prisoner to be released into society. Apparently, this helped to divert the Jews' attention away from their dissatisfaction with the Roman government.

> "Which of the two do you want me to release to you?" asked the governor.
> "Barabbas," they answered.
> "What shall I do, then, with Jesus who is called the Messiah?" Pilate asked.
> They all answered, "Crucify him!"
> "Why? What crime has he committed?" asked Pilate.
> But they shouted all the louder, "Crucify him!"
> When Pilate saw that he was getting nowhere, but that instead an uproar was starting, he took water and washed his hands in front of the crowd. "I am innocent of this man's blood," he said. "It is your responsibility!"
> All the people answered, "His blood is on us and on our children!"
> Then he released Barabbas to them. But he had Jesus flogged, and handed him over to be crucified(Matthew 27:21-26).

The powerful Jewish officials used the excuse of Passover to backhandedly manipulate the governor to release Barabbas so Jesus could take his place. As smart as he was, I wonder if Pilate had an idea about the conspiracy. What I do know is that the Roman governor began to fear the crowd. The Jews started to get loud and angry as the Jewish leaders continued to rile them up. Because he was afraid of what the crowd would do, Pontius Pilate obliged their request.

The high priests were shrewd. They knew exactly what they were doing. Not wanting to be made publically responsible for the death of Jesus, they maneuvered the situation so Jesus would be killed under the direction of the Roman government, not by the Jewish people (the Judean death penalty method was stoning). Pontius Pilate ultimately sentenced Jesus to crucifixion, the death penalty enforced by Roman law.

> "Then the governor's soldiers took Jesus into the Praetorium and gathered the whole company of soldiers around him. They stripped him and put a scarlet robe on him, and then twisted together a crown of thorns and set it on his head. They put a staff in his right hand. Then they knelt in front of him and mocked him. "Hail, king of the Jews!" they said. They spit on him, and took the staff and struck him on the head again and again. After they had mocked him, they took off the robe and put his own clothes on him. Then they led him away to crucify him"(Matthew 27:27-31).

The Cross of Jesus Christ and the Fulfillment of the Law

During his ministry Jesus said, "Do not think that I have come to abolish the Law or the Prophets; I have not come to abolish them but to fulfill them. For truly I tell you, until heaven and earth disappear, not the smallest letter, not the least stroke of a pen, will by any means disappear from the Law until everything is accomplished"(Matthew 5:17-18).

Jesus considered the law and the writings of the prophets important. He knew that his arrest and subsequent death was part of the plan of salvation and therefore had to happen. When Jesus was arrested in the Garden of Gethsemane, Peter came to his defense. The disciple struck the servant of the high priest and cut off his ear. This violent act elicited a rebuke from Jesus.

> "Put your sword back in its place," Jesus said to him, "for all who draw the sword will die by the sword. Do you think I cannot call on my Father, and he will at once put at my disposal more than twelve legions of angels? But how then would the Scriptures be fulfilled that say it must happen in this way?"
> In that hour Jesus said to the crowd, "Am I leading a rebellion, that you have come out with swords and clubs to capture me? Every day I sat in the temple courts teaching, and you did not arrest me. But this has all taken place that the writings of the prophets might be fulfilled." Then all the disciples deserted him and fled(Matthew 26:52-56).

The Old Testament prophets wrote many prophecies concerning the birth, life, and death of Jesus Christ. These examples show how Jesus fulfilled the ancient law.

Matthew 2:5-6 fulfills the prophecy found in Micah. "But you, Bethlehem, in the land of Judah, are by no means least among the rulers of Judah; for out of you will come a ruler who will shepherd my people Israel." Micah 5:2 tells us, "But you, Bethlehem Ephrathah, though you are small among the clans of Judah, out of you will come for me one who will be ruler over Israel, whose origins are from of old, from ancient times."

We read in Matthew 2:15, "...where he stayed until the death of Herod. And so was fulfilled what the Lord had said through the prophet: "Out of Egypt I called my son." This Scripture fulfilled the prophecy found in Hosea 11:1, "When Israel was a child, I loved him, and out of Egypt I called my son."

The prophecy found in Jeremiah 31:15 — "This is what the LORD says, "A voice is heard in Ramah, mourning and great weeping, Rachel weeping for her children and refusing to be comforted, because they are no more" — was fulfilled when Herod the Great ordered the death of all baby boys under the age of two(see Matthew 2:17-18).

When John the Baptist was in prison, he sent for Jesus' disciples. He asked them to ask Jesus if He was really the Messiah. Jesus sent the following message back: "Go back and report to John what you have seen and heard: The blind receive sight, the lame walk, those who have leprosy are cleansed, the deaf hear, the dead are raised, and the good news is proclaimed to the poor. Blessed is anyone who does not stumble on account of me"(Luke 7:22-23). Isaiah 29:18 speaks of this prophecy, "In that day the deaf will hear the words of the scroll, and out of gloom and darkness the eyes of the blind will see."

The messages spoken by God through the Old Testament prophets did not die when they did, but were fulfilled through Jesus Christ. This is why the ancient words of the past are important to us today and will continue to be in the future.

Caligula, the Third Roman Emperor

The New Testament makes no mention of Caligula, the third Roman emperor who ruled from 37 until 41. The Annals, a seven-hundred-page

A Bust of Caligula
Ny Carlsberg Glyptotek

book written by Tacitus, one of Rome's great historians, devotes only four pages to Caligula. One thing he is known for, though, is bankrupting the empire's treasury.

Caligula caused quite a stir among the Jewish people because of his claims of divinity. He erected statutes of himself and demanded that he be worshiped as a god. The Jews became furious at the ludicrous claim and refused to obey the emperor. Around 38, when news of the rebellion reached Rome, an enraged Caligula attempted to deport the Jewish people out of Rome and Alexandria. (At the time, the Egyptian city of Alexandria was the second largest city after Rome and housed more than one million Jews.)

Violence erupted and Philo Judaeus, a Jewish scholar and leader in Alexandria, came to the defense of the Jews. He formed a delegation and asked for a meeting with Caligula to protest the persecution of the Jews. The meeting was pointless. Caligula was significantly late in attending the meeting and while Philo presented his case, the emperor didn't pay much attention to the Jewish representative. Nevertheless, Philo spoke with wisdom, calm, and passion. Soon after, in 41, members of the Praetorian Guard assassinated the emperor.

The Conversion and Ministry of the Apostle Paul

Most of us know the Apostle Paul as the author of most of the New Testament. But prior to becoming a follower of Christ, which historians say occurred around 33-36, Paul (then known as Saul) persecuted Christians and made numerous appeals to the Sanhedrin for permission to arrest followers of Jesus (see Acts 9:2). Paul himself had a close relationship with the Sanhedrin. He was educated by a man called Gamaliel, a Pharisee and one of the three greatest scholars of the law of Judea. Gamaliel was also the chairman of the Sanhedrin and thus held a great deal of power in Judea. These Jewish leaders in the community had high hopes for Paul. I imagine that if the apostle had not been converted through the Gospel, he would have likely followed the same path as Gamaliel and held a high position in the Sanhedrin.

But God changed Paul's life in a remarkable way.

> "Meanwhile, Saul was still breathing out murderous threats against the Lord's disciples. He went to the high priest and asked him for letters to the synagogues in Damascus, so that if he found any there who belonged to the Way, whether men or women, he might take them as prisoners to Jerusalem. As he neared Damascus on his journey, suddenly a light from heaven flashed around him. He fell to the ground and heard a voice say to him, "Saul, Saul, why do you persecute me?"
> "Who are you, Lord?" Saul asked.
> "I am Jesus, whom you are persecuting," he replied. "Now get up and go into the city, and you will be told what you must do."
> The men traveling with Saul stood there speechless; they heard the sound but did not see anyone. Saul got up from the ground, but when he opened his eyes he could see nothing. So they led him by the hand into Damascus. For three days he was blind, and did not eat or drink anything"(Acts 9:1-9).

After spending some time in Damascus, the Apostle Paul began his public ministry. The book of Acts details his three missionary journeys spreading the Gospel. During his second missionary journey, Paul established the first church plant in Europe in the city of Philippi. The book of Acts tells of the genesis of this event and how God specifically called him to preach the gospel to the people of Macedonia.

> "Paul and his companions traveled throughout the region of Phrygia and Galatia, having been kept by the Holy Spirit from preaching the word in the province of Asia. When they came to the border of Mysia, they tried to enter Bithynia, but the Spirit of Jesus would not allow them to. So they passed by Mysia and went down to Troas. During the night Paul had a vision of a man of Macedonia standing and begging him, "Come over to Macedonia and help us." After Paul had seen the vision, we got ready at once to leave for Macedonia, concluding that God had called us to preach the gospel to them. From Troas we put out to sea and sailed straight for Samothrace, and the next day we went on to Neapolis. From there we traveled to Philippi, a Roman colony and the leading city of that district of Macedonia. And we stayed there several days"(Acts 16:6-12).

The historic European evangelism began with Paul healing a slave girl possessed by a demon(see Acts 16:16-21). Consequently, he and his companion Silas were arrested, beaten, and thrown in a prison cell with their feet fastened in stocks. God released them in a dramatic way.

That night, "there was such a violent earthquake that the foundations of the prison were shaken. At once all the prison doors flew open, and everyone's chains came loose. The jailer woke up, and when he saw the prison doors open, he drew his sword and was about to kill himself because he thought the prisoners had escaped. But Paul shouted, "Don't harm yourself! We are all here!" The jailer called for lights, rushed in and fell trembling before Paul and Silas. He then brought them out and asked, "Sirs, what must I do to be saved?" They replied, "Believe in the Lord Jesus, and you will be saved — you and your household." Then they spoke the word of the Lord to him and to all the others in his house"(Acts 16:26-32).

As you can imagine, Paul was frequently confronted with great resistance given his background and the message he preached. The Jewish people in particular did not accept Paul's claim that Jesus was the Messiah and hated the apostle for it. At the beginning of his ministry, they even formed a conspiracy to kill him, which Paul discovered(see Acts 9:23). He was stoned by an angry mob, beaten to the point of death, thrown in prison multiple times, and was the subject of many murder plots. On one occasion, a group of Jewish people even swore they wouldn't eat or drink until Paul was dead (see Acts 23:12-13). I deeply admire the apostle for his courage, his devotion to God, and his commitment to preach the Good News of salvation. (You can read the book of Acts to learn the details of his life.)

Emperor Claudius & Herod Agrippa I

After members of the Senate and the imperial guard assassinated Caligula in 41, his fifty-year-old uncle Claudius (Tiberius Claudius Caesar Augustus Germanicus) immediately took the throne. Until that time, there had been no evidence that he would ever become emperor as he had no political aspirations. He brought with him Pallas, Callistus, and Narcissus, freed Greek slaves who were intelligent and capable leaders, to act as his secretaries.

Claudius was the youngest son of Drusus, the second son born to Livia during her first marriage. From childhood, Claudius suffered from slight

A Marble Head of the Roman Emperor Claudius
The British Museum

paralysis and deafness and a condition that made him produce excessive saliva, which he could not control. Despite his physical challenges, Claudius proved to be an effective and capable ruler. He was also an excellent historian.

While in power, Emperor Claudius appointed Herod Agrippa I, a childhood friend, as the king of all of Judea. Herod Agrippa I had already been granted control over his uncles' territories by Caligula, but when Claudius appointed him ruler over the entire region, Judea finally regained her autonomy and was no longer ruled by a Roman official. It was the first time since Herod the Great's death. The new king was able to make renovations to the temple and the walls of Jerusalem and implement other changes without consulting Rome.

During Claudius's reign as emperor, he relocated the Roman government headquarters from Jerusalem to Caesarea Maritima so the Jewish people could live free without persecution or oppression. The emperor even ordered Roman officials staying in Caesarea not to bring with them any images or symbols of the Roman government whenever they visited Jerusalem.

In 44, Herod Agrippa I died of a mysterious illness. His son, Agrippa II, did not immediately ascend to the throne because he was too young. A Roman procurator was appointed to rule over the province instead. In 48, Claudius appointed Agrippa II as king over a third of his father's territory; however, the Jewish people despised the new king because he was intolerant of Judaism. In 53, the emperor granted Agrippa II the territory that had once belonged to his uncle Philip.

In 49, Emperor Claudius expelled all the Jews from Rome. There was much tension and conflict brewing between Jews who believed Jesus Christ was the Messiah and those who did not. Some historians believe his banishment of them was a way to maintain peace in the region. The Bible mentions this event. "After this, Paul left Athens and went to Corinth. There he met a Jew named Aquila, a native of Pontus, who had recently come from Italy with his wife Priscilla, because Claudius had ordered all Jews to leave Rome. Paul went to see them, and because he was a tentmaker as they were, he stayed and worked with them"(Acts 18:1-3).

Felix, the Roman Governor and the Apostle Paul's Ministry

Before Claudius took the throne, he had been twice divorced. After he became emperor he divorced his third wife and married again. His secretary Pallas convinced Claudius that, for political reasons, he should marry Agrippina, a widow who had a son. The new empress was grateful to Pallas for the recommendation and thanked him by orchestrating the appointment of his younger brother Felix as governor of Judea in 52.

Felix's name in Latin means "lucky one." He came from a family of freed slaves who showed themselves to be capable, intelligent, and successful leaders in the Roman government. Indeed, much luck was upon his family.

When the Apostle Paul returned to Jerusalem after his third missionary journey, he faced a terrible threat to his life. (You can read the full account in Acts 23.) Radical Jews who opposed the apostle had formed a mob and attacked him. Although Roman guards rescued Paul, they also arrested him and put him in chains. Later, when a particular commander became aware that Paul was a Roman citizen, he was horrified at how the apostle had been treated. At the time, Roman citizens were highly respected and had many rights afforded to them, one of which was that they were not allowed to be bound by chains.

The next day, the same commander released Paul, gathered together the chief priests and members of the Sanhedrin, and brought Paul before them. Paul's speech that day caused another tremendous uproar and, for his own safety, Roman guards escorted the evangelist away from the violent, rioting crowd and put him in the barracks. The next morning, yet again, a group of Jews formed a conspiracy to have him killed.

The Romans had plans to escort Paul to Caesarea, but they knew they had to take extra precautions because of how violent the Jews were against him. The commander made arrangements so Paul could safely arrive in the care of Governor Felix, who would hear his case. "Then he called two of his centurions and ordered them, "Get ready a detachment of two hundred soldiers, seventy horsemen and two hundred spearmen to go to Caesarea at nine tonight. Provide horses for Paul so that he may be taken safely to Governor Felix"(Acts 23:23-24). The commander also wrote the governor a letter detailing the situation, and Felix ordered Paul to be kept under watch in the palace(see verses 34-35).

The case was heard a few days later. The courtroom was full of Paul's accusers including the high priest Ananias, the elders of Judea, and an attorney, Tertullus. They implicated him with preaching the gospel of Jesus Christ to the Jewish Diaspora. By that time, Paul's ministry had spread like wildfire.

Tertullus spoke first before Governor Felix, "We have enjoyed a long period of peace under you, and your foresight has brought about reforms in this nation. Everywhere and in every way, most excellent Felix, we acknowledge this with profound gratitude. But in order not to weary you further, I would request that you be kind enough to hear us briefly. We have found this man to be a troublemaker, stirring up riots among the Jews all over the world. He is a ringleader of the Nazarene sect and even tried to desecrate the temple; so we seized him. By examining him yourself you will be able to learn the truth about all these charges we are bringing against him"(Acts 24:3-8).

After Tertullus ended his speech, the governor then told Paul to present his defense. Paul began, "I know that for a number of years you have been a judge over this nation; so I gladly make my defense. You can easily verify that no more than twelve days ago I went up to Jerusalem to worship. My accusers did not find me arguing with anyone at the temple, or stirring up a crowd in the synagogues or anywhere else in the city. And they cannot prove to you the charges they are now making against me. However, I admit that I worship the God of our ancestors as a follower of the Way, which they call a sect. I believe everything that is in accordance with the Law and that is written in the Prophets, and I have the same hope in God as these men themselves have, that there will be a resurrection of both the righteous and the wicked. So I strive always to keep my conscience clear before God and man"(Acts 24:10-16). (The rest of this chapter details the conclusion of Paul's speech.)

After hearing both sides, Felix postponed the case. "Then Felix, who was well acquainted with the Way, adjourned the proceedings. "When Lysias the commander comes," he said, "I will decide your case." He ordered the centurion to keep Paul under guard but to give him some freedom and permit his friends to take care of his needs"(Acts 24:22-23).

The Bible tells us that Governor Felix knew about Jesus Christ(see Acts 24:22) and also respected Paul. Several days later, the governor came with his wife Drusilla, who was Jewish, to visit Paul. The apostle spoke about his faith in Jesus Christ. He continued to talk to them about spiritual matters like righteousness and self-control, and at one point Felix put an end to the conversation. The Bible actually says the governor was frightened. "Go away for now," he replied. "When it is more convenient, I'll call for you again"(Acts 24:25).

While the governor was open to Christianity to a degree, he was still sly. Luke, the writer of Acts, tells us that this Roman official was hoping Paul would offer him a bribe, so he kept Paul in prison and visited him every now and again(see verse 26). If Felix was hoping for a bribe, I gather that Paul either must have had access to a lot of money, probably from the donations he collected, or Felix was your garden-variety scheming politician. Either way, the governor took a pitiful position on the matter. The governor left Paul in prison for two years in order to gain the approval of the Jews. Two years later, Felix was succeeded by Porcius Festus.

Paul's Request for a Trial Before the Emperor

After he became governor, the Jewish leaders presented their case against Paul to Festus, accusing him of many different charges, none of which could be proven. In his defense, Paul told Festus, "I have done nothing wrong against the Jewish law or against the temple or against Caesar" (Acts 25:8). Festus wanted to move the trial from Caesarea to Jerusalem, but Paul refused and exercised his right to appeal.

"Paul answered: "I am now standing before Caesar's court, where I ought to be tried. I have not done any wrong to the Jews, as you yourself know very well. If, however, I am guilty of doing anything deserving death, I do not refuse to die. But if the charges brought against me by these Jews are not true, no one has the right to hand me over to them. I appeal to Caesar!" After Festus had conferred with his council, he declared: "You have appealed to Caesar. To Caesar you will go!"(Acts 25:10-12).

Paul exercised his highest right as a Roman citizen — he asked for his case to be heard in front of the Roman emperor. Being a Roman citizen at the time provided several rights. One of them, similar to the law in the United States, was that one was innocent until properly tried and proven guilty. This is why the commander was so angry that his soldiers had bound Paul upon his arrest; the apostle was, as per the law, innocent. The Hellenistic Empire had deep respect for philosophy. The nation of Israel, religion. The Romans highly valued the law and thus respected those who understood and enacted their legal rights.

The Romans also had an appeal process that went as high up as the emperor. Paul used this legal opportunity to petition his case to be heard in front of Caesar. (It's important to note that "Caesar" in this context stood for "emperor." Nero was the actual emperor of Rome during this time, not Caesar.) Paul was left in prison awaiting trial in Rome. Festus wasn't sure how he should charge Paul and consulted with King Herod Agrippa II for advice. Another hearing was held in front of the Judean king during which Paul gave a lengthy passionate defense. This speech also included testimony of his conversion(see Acts 26:2-23). At the end of the hearing, the king and the governor still couldn't find a reason to keep him in prison, but because Paul had made his appeal to the emperor, he had to remain in jail.

"The king rose, and with him the governor and Bernice and those sitting with them. After they left the room, they began saying to one another, "This man is not doing anything that deserves death or imprisonment."

Cicero denounces Catiline
by Cesare Maccari

Agrippa said to Festus, "This man could have been set free if he had not appealed to Caesar"(Acts 26:30-32). The last two chapters in the book of Acts detail Paul's journey to Rome for his trial before Nero. It makes no mention, however, of the actual trial.

Nero, the Fifth Emperor of Rome

Nero (Nero Claudius Caesar Augustus Germanicus) came into power as emperor in 54 after Claudius was murdered. He was only sixteen years old and, therefore, lacked the kind of wisdom and experience needed to lead an empire. But Nero still acquired this position thanks to his mother, Agrippina. Some historians believe that Agrippina was responsible for the death of her husband as she was known for having a power-hungry appetite and for being ruthless.

The empress desperately wanted her son to inherit the throne of Rome, so she manipulated Claudius into adopting Nero. Agrippina had Nero educated by the great philosopher Seneca. She meddled in every aspect of her son's life. A few years after becoming emperor, Nero had tired of her antics and had her removed from the palace. He then began plotting her murder. It has been recorded that Nero had a boat built for her that was supposed to sink. But his plan failed. She miraculously survived the attempted drowning only to be stabbed to death by assassins in 59.

The Bronze Statue of Nero
The British Museum

Nero loved the arts more than he loved politics, and he especially loved to sing. After his mother's death he began singing in public. He loved the attention. In 64, he made his national debut in Naples. According to The Annals by Tacitus, so many people showed up at the performance that the theatre collapsed.

That same year, Tacitus also wrote that Nero was performing at a concert in Antium when a great fire broke out in Rome and lasted several days. Some historians say that upon his return to Rome during the fire, Nero climbed a rooftop and began singing.

Many of the citizens of Rome thought he intentionally set fire to his city. This rumor spread quickly throughout the city and when Nero caught wind of it, he became upset. Wanting desperately to uphold his innocence, he looked for a scapegoat to blame. The easiest group to target was the Christians. There were many illogical rumors and beliefs about this group of people. For instance, some thought Christians were cannibals because they celebrated the "blood" of Christ during communion. For the next few years, Nero used tortuous and perverse means to kill Christians. The apostles Paul and Peter were two of Nero's victims and were martyred in the name of Christ.

Tacitus wrote, "Besides being put to death they [the Christians] were made to serve as objects of amusement; they were clad in the hides of beast and torn to death by dogs; others were crucified, others set on fire to serve to illuminate the night when daylight failed. Nero had thrown open his grounds for the display, and was putting on a show in the circus, where he mingled with the people in the dress of a charioteer or drove about in his chariot. All this gave rise to a feeling of pity, even toward men whose guilt merited the most exemplary punishment; for it was felt that they were being destroyed not for the public good but to satisfy the cruelty of an individual."[65)]

Unable to withstand his madness and cruelty, Nero's staff abandoned him and the people of Rome launched civil revolts. There was even an assassination conspiracy against him. Unnerved by the chaos, Nero committed suicide in 68. Some historians believe that after Nero's death the Senate passed *damnatio memoriae*, a form of punishment that erases an individual from history. The meaning of the Latin phrase is "condemnation of memory." Roman males considered it to be the greatest disgrace. Thanks to the historian Tacitus and the efforts of early Christians to record Nero's wrongs, we have some history of the moral crimes of this emperor.

The Continuation and End of Roman Persecution

Nero's biggest legacy was the customary persecution of Christians, which continued until 313 when Emperor Constantine legalized Christianity throughout the empire.

Christians suffered greatly for almost 250 years. During this time, many of the authors of the New Testament books risked their lives for the Gospel and wrote letters to believers of the Church to encourage and teach them. The Apostle John wrote Revelation, the last book of the Bible, while exiled by Emperor Domitian, who ruled Rome from 81 to 96. John was imprisoned on an island called Patmos, a quarry mine where many criminals were housed. The prisoners worked in the quarry as laborers, a backbreaking form of physical punishment.

Though there is little historical proof, Emperor Domitian is believed to have persecuted both Jews and Christians alike during his reign. When he was assassinated in 96, the Senate again passed *damnatio memoriae* against him for that reason and others.

The most severe persecution of Christians was under Emperor Diocletian who ruled from 284 to 305. The era came to be called the Great Persecution. Diocletian published an edict against the Christians. He took away the rights of believers and demanded they worship according to Roman religious practices. If Christians did not worship and make sacrifices to the Roman gods, they would be tortured, killed, or sent to prison. It was the darkest hour before dawn.

When Emperor Constantine, known as Constantine the Great, came into power in 306, the direction of religion in the Roman Empire drastically changed. Influenced by his mother who was a believer, Constantine had a religious experience after a particular battle in 312 and converted to Christianity. The following year he issued the Edict of Milan, which declared Christianity legal. Some people questioned the authenticity of his conversion and allege he became a Christian for political reasons. I suppose anything is possible; nonetheless, the emperor is due credit for allowing believers to freely worship God. Constantine reinstated Christians' legal rights and returned to them property and other items that had been confiscated during the persecution.

In addition to his religious reform, one of Emperor Constantine's impressive achievements was building the city of Constantinople. This six-year task of establishing the city as a new capital of Rome was completed in 330. It was this city's capture in 1453 that marked the end of the Roman Empire.

Religious reform in favor of Christians did not end after Emperor Con-

Baptism of Constantine
by Raphael

stantine's death in 377. Emperor Theodosius I, also known as Theodosius the Great, who ruled Rome from 379 to 395, issued the Edict of Thessalonica, which established Christianity as the empire's religion.

The Decline of the Roman Empire

In 285, Diocletian divided up the Roman Empire to be ruled by him and three co-emperors. This tetrarchy lasted until the empire was reunited under Emperor Constantine following a series of civil wars. After Constantine's death, divisions reemerged as a succession of emperors and co-emperors fought for power. When Theodosius I died in 395, the empire was divided for the last time between his sons; Aracdius ruled the East and Honorius the West.

All the power struggles and civil wars that occurred weakened the empire. There is much speculation as to when the Western Roman Empire fell. Some historians believe it occurred in 476. I find it strange that no one knows for sure. It's almost as if it happened unnoticed. The Eastern part of the Roman Empire, however, was destroyed nearly a thousand years later when Sultan Mehmed II of the Ottoman Empire invaded Constantinople in 1453.

The fall of this empire that had existed for over fifteen hundred years was complex and occurred gradually. The reasons for its destruction were many: the government was running out of money; barbarians were invading the territory; the system of choosing an emperor was ineffective; the empire had grown too big too fast and required a high level of political and financial maintenance; and agriculture was declining. Like all empires, Rome began with great ambition but ended up closing her doors.

God's Management of the Universe

The keyword I connect to the Roman Empire is "tolerance." Rome viewed herself as a tolerant empire that was accepting of others. Some of the ancient Roman coins were even inscribed with the word *clementia*, which stands for clemency or mercy. Tolerance, however, is not a legitimate policy simply because the word exists on currency.

Though Rome may have believed they enacted a policy of tolerance and perhaps in some regard had done so — for instance, by allowing Judea to be ruled semi-independently by a Jewish king — the fact is, empires and tolerance do not go hand-in-hand. How can they if empires are rooted in imperialism, acquiring territory and power through forceful means?

True tolerance, mercy, and generosity are found in the cross. Jesus Christ, the Son of God, came to this world to save all mankind, regardless of gender, age, race, background, status, financial situation, education. There is a vast difference between the gestures of charity of man and those of God. Empires, not even one as big as the Roman Empire, can pride themselves on being generous or having admirable policies of tolerance.

* * *

The five empires and Egypt, as illustrated in the Bible, is evidence that the temptation exists for a ruler to greedily expand his empire and even pursue imperialism at all costs. The effort to enlarge territories and gain more power sometimes comes at the price of destroying or oppressing other nations. Instead of respecting the boundaries of others, the leader is blinded by an insatiable hunger for more. We have seen this acted out in the lives of Pharaoh of Egypt, King Sennacherib of Assyria, King Nebuchadnezzar of Babylon, and others.

Through studying these empires, it's clear that God loves people. Throughout the Word, we read how God always promises to take care of His people if they continue to serve them. And even when they don't, but eventually return to Him, He lavishes them with love and forgiveness. Through the nation of Israel, we see how God miraculously saved and delivered His children in spite of powerful empires and the shadows of seemingly impossible circumstances. And we see how God gave the Jewish people chance after chance to repent when they turned away from Him. It's clear that the individual is very precious to God's heart.

When God sent His son, Jesus Christ, to die for our sins, He offered the ultimate example of love. This act illustrates how much God cares and loves us today. How many empires or powerful leaders would do the same? None. Through having a new life in Christ, we also bear ties to the eternal. And empires? Well, we've seen that they last only a short time. Whether they are destroyed by nature, by armies, by famine, by lack of finances, or by other means, every mighty power, organization, or country has an expiration date. Our trust should always rest in the Lord, no matter the size, strength, economic stability, or power of anyone or anything that competes for our attention or devotion.

The impermanent characteristic of empires reminds me of a passage in Psalm. "No king is saved by the size of his army; no warrior escapes by his great strength. A horse is a vain hope for deliverance; despite all its great strength it cannot save. But the eyes of the LORD are on those who fear him, on those whose hope is in his unfailing love, to deliver them from death and keep them alive in famine"(Psalm 133:16-19). It is my hope and prayer that we understand and appreciate the lessons learned from the empires as written about in the Bible. God is more powerful than earthly powers. He is mightier than all earthly might. Kingdoms will rise and fall, but the Lord will last forever. Therefore, may we daily position our trust, our dependence, and our faith only in Him.

Footnote

1) Edward Sayre and Samantha Constant, "The Whole World is Watching," *National Journal*, February 21, 2011.

2) Jongsuh Koo, *Nation and the World: A Resistance of Nationalism toward Imperialism* (Seoul: Nanam, 1988).

3) Byoungho Zoh, *Let's Tong: Ten Thousand Year Old Testament* (Seoul: Tongdokwon, 2011).

4) Paul Johnson, *A History of the Jews* (New York: Harper & Row, 1987).

5) Byoungho Zoh, *Let's Tong: Ten Thousand Year Old Testament* (Seoul: Tongdokwon, 2011).

6) Flavius Josephus, *The Works of Flavius Josephus* trans. William Whiston (New York: John B. Alden, 1891).

7) Arnold C. Brackman, *The Luck of Nineveh: In Search of the Lost Assyrian Empire* (New York: Van Nostrand Reinhold, 1981).

8) Herodotus, *The Histories*, ed. By John M. Marincola, trans. By Aubery de Selincourt (London: Penguin Classics, 2003)

9) Ibid.

10) Arnold C. Brackman, *The Luck of Nineveh: In Search of the Lost Assyrian Empire* (New York: Van Nostrand Reinhold, 1981).

11) Ibid.

12) Ibid

13) Ibid.

14) Ibid.

15) Ibid.

16) The double portion of spiritual power actually means the share of the firstborn. The "double share" noted in Deuteronomy 21:17 is the same Hebrew word as the double portion Elisha asks for.

17) Paul Johnson, *A History of the Jews* (New York: Harper and Row, 1987).

18) Ibid.

19) Ibid.

20) Flavius Josephus, *The Works of Flavius Josephus* trans. William Whiston (New York: John B. Alden, 1891).

21) Ibid.

22) Flavius *Josephus, The Works of Flavius Josephus* trans. William Whiston (New York: John B. Alden, 1891).

23) Ibid.

24) Paul Johnson, *A History of the Jews* (New York: Harper & Row, 1987).

25) Leon J. Wood, *A Survey of Israel's History* (Michigan: Zondervan, 1986).

26) Herodotus, *The Persian War* trans. William Shepherd (Cambridge: Cambridge University Press, 1982).

27) Ibid.

28) Philip de Douza, Waldemar Heckel, Lloyd Llewellyn-Jones, *The Greeks at War: from Athens to Alexander* (Oxford: Osprey Publishing, 2004).

29) Flavius Josephus, *The Works of Flavius Josephus* trans. William Whiston (New York: John B. Alden, 1891).

30) Herodotus, *The Histories* ed. John M Marincola, trans. Aubery de Selincourt (London: Penguin Classics, 2003).

31) Philp de Douza, Waldemar Heckel, Lloyd Llewellyn-Jones, *The Greeks at War: from Athens to Alexander* (Oxford: Osprey Publishing, 2004).

32) Herodotus, *The Histories* ed. John M Marincola, trans. Aubery de Selincourt (London: Penguin Classics, 2003).

33) Flavius Josephus, *The Works of Flavius Josephus* trans. William Whiston (New York: John B. Alden, 1891).

34) Ibid.

35) Leon J. Wood, *A Survey of Israel's History* (Michigan: Zondervan, 1986).

36) Flavius Josephus, *The Works of Flavius Josephus* trans. William Whiston (New York: John B. Alden, 1891).

37) Herodotus, *The Histories* ed. John M Marincola, trans. Aubery de Selincourt (London: Penguin Classics, 2003).

38) Philip de Douza, Waldemar Heckel, Lloyd Llewellyn-Jones, *The Greeks at War: from Athens to Alexander* (Oxford: Osprey Publishing, 2004).

39) Barry Strauss, *The Battle of Salamis: The Naval Encounter that Saved Greece and Western Civilization* (New York: Simon & Schuster, 2004).

40) Jee-Gang Yoon, *The Four Greatest Marine Battles of the World* (Goyang: Books that Have Feeling, 2007).

41) Barry Strauss, *The Battle of Salamis: The Naval Encounter that Saved Greece and Western Civilization* (New York: Simon & Schuster, 2004).

42) Flavius Josephus, *The Works of Flavius Josephus* trans. William Whiston (New York: John B. Alden, 1891).

43) Philip de Douza, Waldemar Heckel, Lloyd Llewellyn-Jones, *The Greeks at War: from Athens to Alexander* (Oxford: Osprey Publishing, 2004).

44) David Aune, *Prophecy in Early Christianity and Ancient Mediterranean Word* (Grand Rapids: Eerdmans, 1983).

45) Philip de Souza, Waldemar Heckel, Lloyd Llewellyn-Jones, *The Greeks at War: from Athens to Alexander* (Oxford, Osprey Publishing, 2004).

46) Ibid.

47) Plutarch, *Plutarch's Lives Volume II*, ed. Arthur High Clough, trans. John Dryen (New York: Random House, 2001).

48) Ibid.

49) Ibid.

50) Philip de Souza, Waldemar Heckel, Lloyd Llewellyn-Jones, *The Greeks at War: from Athens to Alexander* (Oxford, Osprey Publishing, 2004).

51) Ibid.

52) Ibid.

53) Plutarch, *Plutarch's Lives Volume II*, ed. Arthur High Clough, trans. John Dryen (New York: Random House, 2001).

54) Ibid.

55) Flavius Josephus, *The Works of Flavius Josephus* trans. William Whiston (New York: John B. Alden, 1891).

56) Paul Johnson, *A History of the Jews* (New York: Harper and Row, 1987).

57) Fritz M. Heichelheim, Cedric A. Yeo, Allen M. Ward, *A History of the Roman People* (Englewood Cliffs, NJ: Prentice-Hall, 1984).

58) Ibid.

59) Arnold B. Rhodes, *The Might Acts of God* (Richmond: CLC, 1964).

60) Flavius Josephus, *The Works of Flavius Josephus* trans. William Whiston (New York: John B. Alden, 1891).

61) Arnold B. Rhodes, *The Mighty Acts of God* (Richmond: CLC, 1964).

62) Ibid.

63) Paul Johnson, *A History of the Jews* (New York: Harper and Row, 1987).

64) Joachim Jeremias, Jerusalem in the time of Jesus London, S.C.M. Press, 1969

65) Henry Bettenson and Chris Maunder, eds., *Documents of the Christian Church, 3rd. ed.* (Oxford UP, 1999)